My Life in the Wilderness

An Alaskan's Story

By Robert L. Hilliker

D1572689

My Life in the Wilderness

Copyright © 2016 by Robert L. Hilliker

Cover Photo: Karl Stoeber

Other photos by Karl Stoeber noted by a "*" in the caption. Used with permission.

Print version ISBN: 978-0692642634

Print version published by Robert L Hilliker

Ebook version published by:

Alaska Dreams Publishing

www.alaskadp.com

Table of Contents

Dedication

To Betty, who was willing to leave all and come with me to share my dream. You have, in one way or another, shared in all of my adventures in the wilds of Alaska, and you have made our cabin in the wilderness a home. Thank you. I love you.

Foreword

The temperature fell precipitously to negative forty-five degrees even as I embarked upon my journey into the Alaskan wilderness for a yearlong sojourn. That year was 1980 and the month was December, a later start than I had hoped for, and now far colder than this greenhorn mid-western city slicker could have imagined as I made my way along Dry Creek to the cabin site that first night. Now here was true wilderness living at its finest, absent all human convenience and contact except for the soft iridescent glow of an occasional trapper style cabin and the wonderful souls that inhabited them.

This first night of plummeting temperatures caught me off guard in the midst of "setup" when my temporary heat source failed unexpectedly, nearly making my first night in the woods my last night on Earth. The gravity of the situation caused me to bolt through the frigid air to one of those aforementioned soft glowing cabins. It would be three days of sitting by a wood stove before my body returned to its normal core temperature.

It was in those first few days of "warming up" that I met him. The roar of a snow machine approaching the cabin, then sudden stillness: The sound of heavy boots on snowpack approaching the door: Then a thunderous voice at the door of a man I guessed to be rather large, and his first words ringing forever in my memory, "I hear there's a violin player in here!" Then the man attached to that deep voice bent low to clear the door header and stood full height in the room. He looked like a giant in that tiny cabin with his silvery beard glistening under the soft glow of an oil lamp hanging from the rafter above. Also of note, he had a rather large looking pistol in a holster hanging from a cartridge belt loaded with bullets aplenty.

This was my first encounter with Bob Hilliker and it must have created a sensation within somewhere between another near death and a bedwetting experience, because I momentarily lost sight of the fact that he was looking for me. Given the probable scarcity of fiddle players in the region, I squeaked out my confession.

And that's the way it all began for me, that year in a remote cabin on the banks of Dry Creek, getting to know this wonderful man and his precious lady, Betty. This is his story. The life of a Mountain Man at heart, living out his dream in the Alaskan Wilderness.

Joel Boggs

Introduction

Sometimes when my family got together, they would ask me to tell them of my experiences living out here in the Alaskan bush. Our times together were few and far between, however, and someone suggested that maybe I could write them down on paper so everyone could have their own copy.

These writings are the result of their request. It has been a real pleasure for me to remember all of my experiences, both good and bad. It is my sincere hope that my children, grandchildren, great-grandchildren and others will enjoy reading about my adventures in the wilds of Alaska.

The author writing in his cabin, 2014

1 The Early Years

My story begins in Battle Creek, Michigan, where I was born in the year nineteen hundred and twenty-eight. The following year my parents moved to Grand Rapids, Michigan, where my brother James (Jim) was born in the year nineteen hundred and thirty. Our parents divorced in 1931, and Jim and I went to live with our Grandma and Grandpa Hilliker. We lived with them until the spring of 1937.

Jim and Bob in Grand Rapids, 1933

In the latter part of April, or the first part of May that year, Grandma called Jim and I to her bedside, and told us that he and I would be going to live with our mother and step-dad, Raymond Walter. They lived in Owosso Michigan, which was about eighty miles east of Grand Rapids. I was nine years old, and Jim was seven. Of course we didn't understand, and in those days people didn't explain things to children. So we didn't ask any questions; we just did what we were told to do.

I did ask Grandma what we should call our step-dad, since he wasn't our real father. She told us to call him "Daddy Raymond" so that's what we called him for a few years, then we just called him Dad. A few days later, they came and loaded our stuff in the car, and we left. I knew that Grandma spent a lot of time in bed, but I didn't know why.

About a month after Jim and I moved to Owosso, we got word that Grandma had passed away. She died of cancer. My mother and step-dad took us to her funeral. Grandpa died three years later, but we were not notified, so of course, could not go to his funeral.

In the summer of 1940 my father came one afternoon to Owosso to see us, and to tell us that Grandpa had passed away in April of that year. My father was living in California at the time, and he didn't receive word of Grandpa's passing either, until after he was already buried.

I felt like Grandma and Grandpa were the only "parents" that I ever had. I was only three years old, and Jim was one and a half when we went to live with them. They took Jim and me in, despite their old age, to give us a home and care for us. In thinking about it all after I got older; I believe they took us in to keep us in the family, and to spare us from going to a foster home. We loved them and we knew that they loved us, and it was a very sad thing for us to know that they were both gone.

After we grew up, Jim and I made a trip to Grand Rapids to find Grandma and Grandpa's graves. We were able to find them, and for several years after that we went over there on Memorial Day thinking that someone might come to put flowers on their graves, and maybe we could find out more about our family. No one ever showed up, however, and we were left with many unanswered questions about our family and our past.

My mother and stepdad were living in a small apartment, and it soon became evident that we needed more room. He acquired some land just inside the western city limits of Owosso, and he and my stepbrother built a twenty-four by thirty-four foot, two-story house. We two boys had a bedroom upstairs. When the house was finished and we got moved in, we had a chance to go through our stuff.

I don't know who packed my stuff, but I discovered my coin bank had not been packed. That was very discouraging to me because I had 97 cents in that bank. Now, I realize that by today's standards, 97 cents doesn't mean much, but in those days you could buy a large, double-dip ice cream cone for a nickel, so that 97 cents represented a lot of ice cream cones. But, I digress. On with my story.

My dad had purchased somewhere around five acres of land. Most of the land, except where the house sat, and where the future garage and a chicken coop would be, was plowed up and fitted for planting. He planted potatoes, corn, tomatoes, beets, carrots, turnips, cucumbers, rutabagas, several kinds of squash, pumpkins, strawberries, and more. We had all we could use, and a whole lot more, so he sold a lot of vegetables to the grocery stores.

He also had a very large flower garden. There were flowers of every color and description. I really liked that flower garden. He also planted a couple apple trees, a peach tree and a cherry tree, but that flower garden with its various colors, all blending in together, was so beautiful.

I still marvel at the beauty of God's creation. The beautiful blue skies, the vast fields of grain, the high and lofty purple snowcapped mountains, and the abundant luscious fruit of the fertile land: America, America, God certainly has shed His grace upon you. The mountains, the valleys, the rivers and creeks that course through them as they meander here and there, eventually finding their way to the ocean, the most beautiful and diverse wild flowers and foliage of our great land, and especially of the "North Country" are awesome to me!

As you can imagine, such a large garden required a lot of work. We used all hand tools to work it such as hoes and cultivators. The soil was yellow clay. When it was dry it was as hard as a rock, and when it was wet, it stuck to everything like glue. When we came out of the garden, we had great globs of the stuff clinging to our shoes. Jim and I spent most of our summer vacations out there. It was alright though, because we always had lots of food to eat, and we liked being outdoors in the fresh air and sunshine.

Bob and Jim in Grand Rapids, 1936

2 The Beginning of the Dream

We lived on the outskirts of town where the houses were scattered around, the closest house to us was a block away. Jim and I had lots of room to wander and explore whenever the opportunity arose. Our dad had a few guns, and he hunted pheasants, cottontail rabbits and deer.

I was very interested in guns and hunting. When I was about fourteen years old, he let me use his single shot 16-gauge shotgun and I started hunting. A couple of years later, Jim also started hunting. We spent many happy hours hunting, and just being free to enjoy the fields and woods.

In those days (the late 1930's and early 1940's) some of the farmers still shocked their corn in the fields and brought it up to the barn later to husk and shell it. They cut the corn stalks and stood a bunch of them up together and tied a piece of binder twine around the top to hold them. This method kept the ears of corn up off the ground and kept them dry. It also kept them up out of the snow in case it was later in the winter before they could bring them in. They called them shocks and they looked like a field full of little teepees.

When the farmers brought the corn into the barn, all of the neighbors would come over and help husk it, and they would have a party called a "husking bee." They also had a hand turned device called a "sheller" which separated the kernels of corn from the cobs.

These corn shocks were great places for cottontails to get in out of the weather. There was just such a place about a mile north of our house. One of us would stand ready to shoot, the other would kick the shocks, and the rabbits came busting out!

I remember one New Year's Day we decided to go rabbit hunting. It was snowing and the wind was blowing. Not the best of weather to be out in, but we rarely ever let the weather stop us if we wanted to do something. The Ann Arbor railroad tracks ran by several hundred yards from our house, and many times we would walk down the tracks hunting. Even though it was a very stormy day, we got more rabbits that day than on days when the weather was a lot nicer. We loved hunting. Sometimes even on school days we would get up early and hunt pheasants before school.

Jim and Bob in Owosso, 1938

During those years, I read stories about Daniel Boone, Jim Bowie and other frontiersmen. Trailblazers they were, explorers, men who just had to "see what was over the next hill," men who opened the country up for others who would follow in their footsteps. In the following years, I also read of the Mountain Man Jim Bridger, who, in his later years, operated a trading post on Black's Fork of the Green River in southwestern Wyoming. I read of Jim Baker, who had the distinction of having the only two-story log cabin in the whole Rocky Mountains.

I read of Hugh Glass, who survived a severe mauling by a grizzly bear. Left by his companions for dead, he did survive and made his way to a fort some miles away. I read of Jedediah Smith, who died at a waterhole, killed by Indians, at the age of thirty-two years. I read of Bill Williams, William Sublette, Joe Meek the "merry mountain man" and others who left the comforts and relative safety of civilization, and ventured into the Great Rocky Mountains to trap beaver. They built log cabins and hunted for their food. They were men who lived free; fiercely independent men who wandered where they pleased, and wherever the beaver would lead them. They were a whole different breed of men: fearless; self-sufficient; able.

As a young boy, their stories stirred something deep within me, touched something in me that I couldn't put into words. As I grew older, the desire to experience such a life for myself only grew stronger: to go into the wilderness, build a strong and warm log cabin with my own two hands, and hunt for my food. Trap fur bearing animals to sell to the fur buyers for money to buy the things I couldn't produce myself, get my water from the creek, cut the firewood I would need to cook my food and to keep me warm through the long cold winters of the "North Country," could *I* do something like that?

Bob (center) with his brother, mother and stepfather in Owosso, 1943

3 Setting Out on My Own

In April of 1946 I joined the U.S. Navy. I was only seventeen years old, so my mother had to sign for me. I spent two years in the North Atlantic and the Mediterranean Sea.

Bob with brother Jim, 1946

Upon returning to Owosso in 1948, I got a job at the Buick automobile plant in Flint, Michigan. It didn't take long for me to realize that I didn't want to spend all of my working years in that hot, smelly place!

Bob and Jim with their mother in Vanderbilt circa 1948

I left there and got a job in Owosso working for Culligan Soft Water Company. My job was servicing soft water tanks in private homes. I serviced about fifty homes a day. I liked the job, but for some reason the foreman didn't like me. It was not a good situation, so I decided to find another job.

I got a job in a factory that made small electric motors. I started out stocking an assembly line. After about a year, I was promoted to the grinding machines, grinding rotors and field cores. I liked the job okay, but it was inside work, and also a job that I didn't want to spend the rest of my life doing. I felt "boxed in" and I wanted out!

One day when we were having our coffee break, I was sitting outside talking with an older man who had been working there for a long time. I mentioned to him that someday I wanted to move "up north." I told him how I loved to be out in the woods, how I loved deer hunting, and that I would like to live where I could be there in minutes instead of hours. He asked, "When are you going to do that, Bob?" I replied, "Oh, I don't know, someday." He said, "Bob, take a tip from me, do it now — otherwise you'll wake up some morning and find yourself to be an old man, like me, and it will be too late." I thought about what he said and decided it was good advice.

While I was in the Navy, my mother and dad had moved to a place a couple of miles north of Vanderbilt, which is in the northern lower peninsula of Michigan. My dad was a carpenter and worked for a small general contracting company in Gaylord, Michigan about ten miles south of where he lived. I wrote to him and told him that I would like to move up north, and if the company he worked for needed more help, to please let me know.

Sometime later on a Friday afternoon when I got home from work, there was a telegram from him stating that the company was going to hire more men, and that if I was still interested, to be up there the next morning for an interview. Well, that was good news. It was only 170 miles up there, so I loaded my wife and little children (my son Robert was 2 1/2 years old and my daughter Eileen was 1 1/2 years old) in the car and took off.

I went into the office the next morning and talked with the manager. He said he wanted me to work for them and asked me if I could start the following Monday morning. I asked him if he could give me a week to move up, because if I was going to work there, I wanted to live there! He said, "Okay, see you a week from Monday." We got moved up that next week and I went to work. It was great. It was mostly outside work, lots of fresh air and sunshine.

I started out as an apprentice carpenter in June of 1953. After a few years, my boss approached me with an offer. He said he had a gas/service station to build, and he wanted me to run the job. I told him that I didn't know anything about reading blueprints or running a job but he said he would help me and that he wanted me to take the job. I told him that if he would help me, I would do my best to get the job done. That job turned out well, and from then on I oversaw more jobs such as schools, medical care facilities, State Police posts, banks, and private homes. I really enjoyed building things and worked for them for 21 years.

Moving to the northern part of Michigan's Lower Peninsula, about fifty miles below the Straits of Mackinac, was all that I had hoped it would be. In just minutes from where I lived I could be out in the woods where I hunted deer. There were black bears, ruffed grouse, squirrels, and rabbits to hunt also.

Thinking of someday living in the "wilderness," I tried my hand at snaring rabbits and did a little trapping. I made rabbit snares out of stranded picture wire. I made a small loop on one end, ran the other end through it, and tied it to a small tree next to a rabbit trail. For rabbits, you make about a 5 to 7 inch loop, and place it in the center of the trail, about 6 inches above the ground. The idea is that the rabbit will get his head in the loop as he comes down the trail and when the loop tightens up he can't get out. They worked very well.

I used #2 and #3 long spring steel traps for fox and coyotes. I'd look for a trail they were using, or a place I thought they would come to, then put some bait or lure on a bush or a tree near the trail and place the trap so that when they came up to investigate the bait they would step on the trap. There are many methods and ways of doing this, and one has to experiment a little to discover what works best for them.

I've heard of folks who think that you put the bait on the pan of the trap, like you would a mousetrap! Sorry, it won't work. That is bad information. If you do it in that way, the animal will smell the trap and dig it up, and you've lost a valuable fur. The trap has to be absolutely odorless.

In the wintertime, I enjoyed going out on my snowshoes. When my son Robert was small, I sometimes took him with me. He stood on the snowshoes behind me and held on to my coat. We both really enjoyed that. Other than our snowshoe trail, there were absolutely no other signs of human presence. Occasionally, we would see a deer track, a grouse exploding up out of the snow, or a lone fox or coyote track lining out across an open place. I loved it all. This was the closest thing I had ever experienced that at least seemed like "wilderness."

My family and I spent a lot of time in the woods in the summer and fall of the year. Often, when I left for work in the morning I would ask my wife to have a picnic lunch prepared, and when I got home from work we would all pile in the car and head for the woods. We roasted hot dogs, had sandwiches and something to drink. We all enjoyed those times. Sometimes we would go swimming in a nearby lake. We would usually finish the day driving around the many two-track trails looking for deer.

There were also old apple orchards scattered through the woods. They were remnants, I suppose, of the many logging camps from the days when they logged off the great white pines that were so plentiful in the northern part of the Lower Peninsula of Michigan. We could usually find some pretty good apples too, if we could get there ahead of the deer and raccoons. Of course, this kind of life served to "fire up" that deep desire in me to live in the wilderness.

4 The '59ers

In 1959, there was a fellow who had been to Alaska, and who came back to Michigan all "fired up" and wanted to lead a group of people back to Alaska. The '59ers, they called themselves. I'm not sure how he got the word out, maybe by word-of-mouth or articles in the newspaper. However he did it, he managed to get quite a following. I think that most of them came from the southeastern part of Michigan.

The main attraction was homesteads. A person could file on land in certain areas, and if you fulfilled all of the requirements, which took several years, you could obtain the Title, or a Patent, as it's called in Alaska, to 160 acres of land. Another attraction was the fact that Alaska became the 49th State of the Union that year.

The '59ers left in all sorts of vehicles, loaded down with furniture and just about everything else that you could imagine. I think that is when the slogan, "Alaska or Bust" got started. Many of them had those big signs on the back of their rigs. Some of them never got out of Michigan before their rigs "busted" and they had to turn back. For years after that time, people headed for Alaska had those signs on the backs of their rigs. My son-in-law Ed put signs on their rig and so did we! Some of the '59ers did make it all the way, but hearsay has it that most of them were pretty disappointed. I heard that some of them did get homesteads, some of them settled in the Matanuska Valley, some settled in Anchorage, and some returned to Michigan.

Someone wrote a song about that time entitled "North to Alaska." I guess you can imagine what affect this all had on me. That same year, I wrote to the Chamber of Commerce in Anchorage requesting information about the cost of living, job opportunities, wages, etc. I received a lot of information from them, but they also strongly suggested that I not even consider coming to Alaska unless I had confirmed employment. I did not, so that was the end of the matter, at least for the time being. I got discouraged a few times, but I never gave up hope of seeing my dream come true.

5 The Flintlock Rifle

In 1968 I met Russ, an x-ray technician in the local hospital who was involved in building muzzle-loading guns. Russ also belonged to several black powder shooting clubs and lived as much as possible in civilization the life of a Mountain Man. I had always been interested in muzzle-loading guns, especially the early flintlock rifles. Maybe it was reading about the mountain men and their guns and what they were able to do with them, or maybe it was just my love for firearms.

Russ and his dog Czar

I asked Russ if he would help me build a flintlock rifle, and he agreed. I would do all of the actual work, but he would instruct me and make suggestions as the job progressed. He helped me choose the style and caliber that I liked, helped me pick out the parts from a catalog that he had and got me started. I just had a small workbench in a back room, but it was sufficient for this job.

As I progressed, he followed through with more guidance and instructions. I was really enjoying this. Russ and I became very good friends and attended many Mountain Man shoots and other festivities together. He and his son, Mike, and I often went out in the woods on weekend camp-outs together. We shot our rifles, threw our tomahawks, and sometimes we just relaxed, enjoying the out-of-doors. Russ made delicious biscuits, and we always had some strawberry jam with us!

I'll add some background here about the gunsmiths of Pennsylvania. The German gunsmiths who settled there each had their own style of building guns. They were recognized by their name, of course, and the county they lived in. A few examples include Bedford County, Bucks County, and Lancaster County. Usually just by looking at the gun—the shape of the stock, the design of the lock mechanism, trigger guard, side plates, and the carving of the stock—you could tell who made the gun.

The year was 1970. The result of all my hard work was a flintlock rifle of .45 caliber, with a ⅞ inch by 43-inch straight octagon barrel. I bought the lock, cast brass buttplate, trigger guard, and side plate because I had no way of making those, but I made the ramrod ferrules, toe plate and nose cap myself from sheet brass. The stock was curly maple, which I purchased in plank form. I drew the shape of the stock on it and did all of the shaping of that with saws, files and wood rasps.

.45 Caliber Flintlock Rifle and Accoutrements

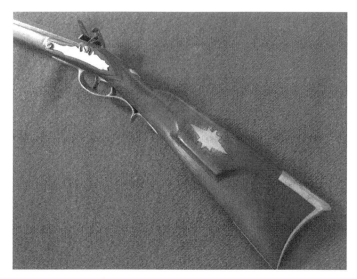

Bob's first Flintlock .45 caliber rifle

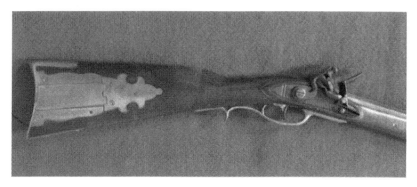

The Patchbox and Lock of the .45 Caliber Rifle

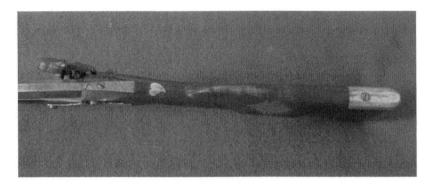

Inlaid 'Weeping heart' on the Flintlock

It was a beautiful piece to behold — at least to me. I poured just the right amount of 3F black powder down the barrel, followed that with a patched lead ball seated firmly on the powder charge, primed the pan with 4F black powder, and cocked the hammer (which was called a "cock" in the old days). How thrilling it was when I pulled the trigger and it fired!

I want to add a few words of caution here. Never, ever use modern smokeless gunpowder in a muzzle-loading gun! Use black powder only! Also in loading a muzzleloader, always be sure that the patched ball is seated firmly on the powder charge! One way to do that is to load your gun, make sure the ball is seated firmly on the powder charge, and put a mark on the ramrod at the muzzle of the gun and make sure that every time you load the gun, the ramrod goes in to that mark. If you break these two rules, you could blow the gun up—ruining it, of course, and the shooter could be seriously injured!

One of the muzzle-loading clubs we belonged to was the "Bear River Firelocks". There were also "Buller Valley" and "The Grand Traverse Métis" Clubs. The Métis were mixed bloods of Canada who were hunters and trappers. Along with our monthly get-togethers, we took part in various goings-on all over the northern part of Michigan's Lower Peninsula.

Some of the Clan of the Grand Traverse Métis

While taking part in these things we all wore period clothing. Some of the women wore the long dresses and bonnets of the early days. The men's costumes were of every material and description. Betty made a wool rifleman's shirt and pants for me, a deer skin dress for herself, and costumes for the kids too. A young buck skinner friend made a coonskin hat for me from a coonskin I had. We also made moose hide moccasins for the whole family. It was like going back in time a couple of hundred years.

Besides the flintlock rifle that I had built earlier, we made all of our own accoutrements: powder measures, powder horns, patch knives, and shooting pouches. We molded our own rifle balls and made various other pieces of equipment.

One time we were invited to a celebration on Mackinac Island. It is a small island at the Northern end of Lake Huron in the Straits of Mackinac. When we arrived there, the weather was nice, but about halfway through the parade, it began to rain. Well! We old Mountain Men weren't about to let a little rain stop us! Of course, it wasn't just men; there were women and children too.

Nevertheless, we kept right on going. We got soaking wet. One very funny thing that happened was that our moose hide moccasins got wet and started to stretch out. The longer we walked, the longer our moccasins got. They stretched out to about two inches longer than our feet. It was difficult to walk, but we got a lot of laughs out of that. Well, anyway, we finished the parade and had a lot of fun. We canceled the shooting match though.

Bob and wife Betty in costume

Another time we were invited to Honor, Michigan—a little town near Traverse City. They were having their Centennial Celebration. There was a big parade, some activities for the kids, and lots of food. We put on a muzzle loading shoot, and knife and tomahawk demonstrations.

One thing that the people liked was that we always took some time to answer questions about our rifles and other accoutrements, and to let spectators who were interested try their hands at throwing the tomahawk. Many were surprised at how easy it was to stick them in the block, once it was explained to them. It really is not difficult; the main thing is distance from the target and throwing consistently every time.

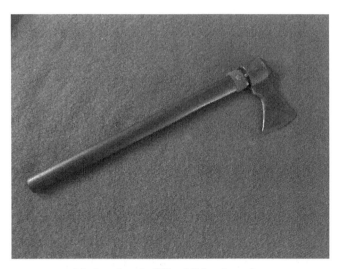

My handmade "Hawk" for throwing

People were surprised at how accurate our rifles were. I guess they thought that since they are muzzleloaders patterned after the Revolutionary War and the Mountain Men's rifles they wouldn't be accurate. There is an old account of a time when the Spaniards occupied Florida. The commander of a fort there, in corresponding with his homeland of Spain, complained that their local enemies were picking off his guards at 400 yards with flintlock rifles.

After the festivities were over at Honor, the folks treated us to a showing of a Mountain Man movie, "Jeremiah Johnson" at their local outdoor theater. It's a movie about a Mountain Man also called "Liver Eatin' Johnson" whose Indian wife and baby were killed by a band of Crow Indians, and his revenge on the Crows. He was also called "Crow Killer." Whenever he killed a Crow Indian, he ate some of his liver! The movie doesn't show that part however. He fought a one-man war against the Crows and finally prevailed. They sent many of their best warriors, one at a time, to kill him—but none succeeded so they finally gave up.

One of the old Mountain Men in the movie told Jeremiah that if it had been some other tribe, they would have sent many after him at the same time. But the Crow way was more honorable, and they only sent one warrior at a time. The movie has some really beautiful footage of mountains and valleys in the Great Rocky Mountains. I've seen that movie many times since then.

The muzzle-loading clubs we belonged to were like most other clubs, in that people who are interested in the same things get together and do "their thing." We usually had a meeting once a month. We shot our rifles and pistols, threw knives and tomahawks at targets, and participated in various other activities relating to the Mountain Man era. It was good friendly competition, and there was always lots of good food. There were things for children to do also, and in fact some of the older kids were learning to shoot and do all the things that the adults were doing. This was something the whole family could do together.

We also had what we called "novelty" shoots. Instead of just punching holes in paper targets all the time, someone would donate a knife, powder horn or something else they had made or purchased. They would tie a string on it, and hang it over a stump or block of wood. Whoever shot and cut the string won the prize. We shot this type of match at a distance of about 15 yards. Sometimes they tied a balloon on a swinging stick. You had to shoot and break the balloon before the stick stopped swinging. This match was shot at 25 yards.

We "snuffed" candles too; if you shot the ball close enough to the flame, it would snuff it out. But, if you hit the candle you were disqualified. If your shot was too high, it didn't snuff the flame out. We shot these matches at about 15 yards also. Sometimes we did the candle snuffing at night. It's more of a challenge, but it can be done.

Another thing we did was to stick a double bitted axe in the end of a log and fasten one clay target on each side of the axe. If your rifle ball hit the edge of the blade, it would split and break both targets. If you didn't hit the edge of the blade it would only break one of them. These are just a few of the things we did besides marching in parades and putting on shooting demonstrations.

Concerning the accuracy of our rifles, I remember one time when we were at a Boy Scout Camp putting on a shooting demonstration. There were about 15 shooters. The distance we were shooting was 25 yards at paper targets. There were two shooters who ended up in a tie for first place. To break the tie, instead of shooting at another paper target, the Chief went down to the target area, took his knife and cut a piece of bark off a branch of a small tree. The branch was about three-quarters of an inch in diameter.

The shooter who cut the branch right at that spot would win the match. The first guy shot, but missed the branch. The second guy shot, and cut the branch off right on that spot. We shot all of the matches' off-hand and used only open sights. I don't think that someone with a modern scoped rifle could do any better than that. There was always a lot of good-natured kidding at those times too. Most of the folks were really nice people and we enjoyed getting together.

Another time we were shooting at Traverse City, with the Grand Traverse Métis. I was doing well that day and it looked like I was going to win. The prize for first place was a jug of Kentucky Bourbon. They knew that I didn't drink alcohol, so the Chief took the jug home, dumped the whiskey out and filled the jug with apple cider. Well, I won the match, and I want to tell you, that was absolutely the best apple cider I had ever tasted!!! Maybe he didn't get quite all of the whiskey out? It's a really neat jug, and I still have it.

6 The Dream Takes Shape

The year was 1973. My wife, Betty, and I were married in April of that year. My three children from a previous marriage had grown up and were on their own. My son Robert was married, as was Eileen, my oldest daughter. Janet, my youngest daughter, was in the Marine Corps.

Betty had three children still at home; Diana 15, Pam 14, and Brian 11. Betty knew of my desire to live in the wilderness, and we had discussed the possibility of moving to Alaska. At first, we talked of moving to the Upper Peninsula of Michigan, which was sparsely populated with lots of room and wild places, but we finally decided that if we were going to move somewhere, we would go all the way — to Alaska!

Bob and Betty in Michigan, 1973

I guess we were doing more wishing than planning. We had no idea what part of Alaska we would go to, or where I could find work, and we didn't have enough money to buy a home, so in light of all of that, we put it on the proverbial shelf for a while. Meanwhile, my daughter Eileen and her husband Ed were thinking of making a move with their little daughter, Amy. I guess all the talking Betty and I had been doing about Alaska was having an effect on them. They decided they were going to move to Alaska and would be leaving around May 1st.

Suddenly, all of this began taking shape in my mind. I was temporarily laid off. This was it! This was my chance...a chance to at least see Alaska. Betty could not go. She had a responsible position with a grocery store chain and she could not be away for a month. I told Ed and Eileen that if they wanted me to, I could haul some of their stuff in my pickup and go with them to Alaska. They said that would be good, and I started getting my stuff together.

Ever hear of Murphy's Law? A couple of days later I got a letter from the company I worked for, asking me to return to work the following Monday morning. That letter sure took the wind out of my sails, but I was not about to give up so easily!

Some winters we didn't have much work, and we would be laid off for a couple of months. I knew that they wanted to keep me working as much as possible, and even if there wasn't a whole lot of work sometimes they would call me back early.

I went over to the office and mentioned that I had received their letter asking me to return to work. I asked Walt, my boss, if he could manage without me for a month. He thought for a moment and said, "Well, I guess so. Why?" I told him of my planned trip to Alaska, and that if he could manage it, I sure would like to go. He said, "Okay. See you the 1st of June." What a relief!

Ed and Eileen had something come up and told me that they wouldn't be able to leave on May 1st. I decided that I'd better go anyway, especially now that I had a deadline to meet. I had to be back by June 1st so I had to get on my way.

To say that I was excited about my trip to Alaska is putting it mildly. All I could think about was getting started. I had a whole month off work, and I was anxious to be on my way. I went about getting my gear packed up, got my truck serviced, and told my family goodbye. I drove west from our house to Old US 27, turned north to Gaylord and turned west on Michigan Highway 32 to Interstate 75, turned north again, and I was on my way.

Before I left home, Betty packed up a big batch of sandwiches and a thermos of coffee. I could stop at a restaurant and get my thermos filled, and those sandwiches lasted me almost to Canada. I would be eating light because I wasn't burning very many calories just riding in the truck.

I had mixed emotions, and my mind was spinning with excitement and anticipation. It was about fifty miles to the Straits of Mackinac. That's where Lake Michigan and Lake Huron meet. In the old days, there was a ferry that operated between Mackinaw City on the south and St. Ignace on the north side of the lake. A few years later, they built a bridge. At the time it was the longest single span suspension bridge in the world. It was five miles across.

At St. Ignace, I turned west on US Highway 2, which would take me across the Upper Peninsula of Michigan, northern Wisconsin, Minnesota, and two thirds of the way across North Dakota to Minot. From there I went northwest on Highway 52 to Portal, ND, and the southern border of Saskatchewan, Canada. I drove through Regina, Saskatoon and North Battleford to Lloydminster, on the border of Alberta, Canada.

On my way through Lloydminster, I saw a sign pointing to a museum. I like museums and needed a break from staring out of the windshield of my truck, so I decided to check it out. The museum was owned by a man who in his earlier years had lived in the wilderness of northern Saskatchewan in a log cabin that he had built himself. The museum was filled with artifacts of his life there. He told me he had hired a taxidermist to mount the various birds and animals that were on display, but he was not satisfied with his work so he learned how to do it himself.

One scene was especially interesting to me. He told me that it happened right outside his cabin. He heard a ruckus outside and looked out his front window to see what was going on. Three wolves had a deer cornered between them. The deer was down on its knees and in real trouble. He grabbed his rifle and shot all three wolves. He had to shoot the deer too because he could see that it could not survive its wounds. He could always use some fresh meat, so it wasn't wasted. He skinned them out and mounted them in the same position that they had been in, and reproduced the scene in his museum.

I was the only visitor there at the time, so he walked around with me and explained the displays of wildlife, and tools etc., of his life in the woods, and he also told me the stories that went with them. One article he had on display was a birch bark cone. It was about 18″ long. The small end was about 1½″, and the large end about 6″. He told me that it was a moose call, explained how to use it, and even demonstrated it for me. He smiled and said that if I was using it and a big bull came toward me, I'd better have my rifle ready because the only way he could be stopped was to shoot him. We looked over the rest of the museum together. There were lots of interesting things there but I had to be on my way. I thanked him for taking the time to show me around. I really enjoyed my time there, and it was one of the highlights of my trip.

A few years before all of this, I was working on a job about sixty-five miles from home. I was staying at a motel and had nothing to do in the evening. I got the idea to build a topper on my pickup. I really had no special reason other than a dry place to carry my tools. I cut two-by-twos for framing and covered it with one-half inch textured plywood. The roof had just a little slope toward each side for the water to run off. I also built a walk-in door in the back (well, a crawl-in door would be a better description).

There was a bench on each side so I could lay a piece of plywood across on top of them to make a bed and have a storage place for my tools underneath. An air mattress and a sleeping bag completed a sleeping space, if I ever needed one. There was a window in each side and one in the back door. I had no idea at the time how handy that would be. I was able to avoid motels on my trip to Alaska. All I had to do was find a campground, or even a gravel pit, and I could spend the night comfortably, and free of charge.

Another highlight of my trip was at Dawson Creek, British Columbia. It was milepost "0", the beginning of the Alaska Highway. From there it is about 1,520 miles to Fairbanks, Alaska.

7 The Alaska Highway

Well, it was very exciting to actually be on the Alaska Highway. Fort St. John was the next town. The highway was paved for a few miles north of Fort St. John, but then it was gravel all the way to the Alaska border, except for a few miles near Whitehorse, Yukon Territory, which was blacktop. The road was continually graded and maintained so traveling was good. One bad feature of the road, however, was that there were no shoulders. The road was narrow, and there was no place to pull over. If you had a flat tire you had to just stop where you were and fix it.

About 175 miles north of Dawson Creek is the Buckinghorse River and campground. I pulled in there late one evening. I was sitting at a picnic table just relaxing when a guy in an old pickup truck drove in and parked a little way from me. He came over and introduced himself. His name was Dennis and he was from Wisconsin. He also was on his way to Alaska. He said he had friends in Anchorage, and planned to spend some time with them.

Dennis told me he had left home in a nice car, but somewhere in Alberta, Canada, some drunks had rear-ended him and totaled it. So, there he was with no transportation. He met an elderly man and his wife who lived nearby, and they offered him a place to stay while he was deciding what to do. Of course he still wanted to get to Alaska, no question about that. They had an old 1952 pickup truck that they offered to sell him. Well, at least it was transportation, so he bought it.

Now, you may think that it was just coincidence that we both stopped at that same campground that evening, but the way things turned out I don't think so. We talked awhile and then headed to our trucks to get some sleep. The next morning, we were both up early and anxious to get going. He came over to me and said he had a thought in the night, and wondered if, since we were both traveling alone, we could travel along together. His truck was old and he didn't know how dependable it was, and if either of us had a problem, we could help each other out. That sounded like a good idea, so that's what we did.

I told him that I planned to head out and stop at the first restaurant that I came to and have some breakfast. He said that he was going to fix his own, but that he would come along and when we stopped he would have his breakfast and then come inside too. It was about fifteen miles up the highway to Trutch Mountain, the second highest summit on the Alaska Highway, at 4,134 feet above sea level. From the top of Trutch Mountain, there was a great view of the British Columbia Rocky Mountains. We would later be driving right through them.

It was another fifty miles or so to the Prophet River, where there was a café. We pulled in and I went inside. There were several other folks in the café, including a young couple with a little boy seated a couple of tables away. I'm not too outgoing when it comes to talking to strangers, so I just ate my breakfast. Dennis, on the other hand, was quite outgoing, and when he came in he struck up a conversation with them. Their names were Doug and Donna and Jimmy. They were from South Carolina and were also on their way to Alaska. Doug was a preacher, and a church in Tok had asked him to be their pastor. We all visited for a while, then Dennis and I got up to leave. Doug mentioned that we might meet again in Tok. Yes, maybe we would.

Right here I want to tell you another story about an incident that took place while we were traveling the Alaska Highway. We stopped at a campground one evening, and during our conversation Dennis asked me if I like pancakes. I told him I did, and he said, "Okay, we'll have pancakes for breakfast." He told me that while he was staying with the folks in Alberta, the lady showed him how to make pancakes without baking powder and he was anxious to try it out.

Early the next morning he got a fire going and was mixing up the pancake dough. I sat down at the picnic table and in a few minutes he had a couple ready. Boy was I ready for this. He had bacon frying too. What a breakfast. I put a pancake on my plate, slathered it with butter, drowned it in syrup, grabbed my fork and proceeded to have my breakfast. "Uh Dennis, Uh, I can't cut this

40

pancake with my fork." "Try your knife," he answered. I tried my knife. "Uh, Dennis, I can't cut it with my knife either." He came over and looked at my problem. He thought for a few seconds and said, "Hmm, I guess I must have forgotten something!"

There are always "camp robbers" around campgrounds and that day was no different. As soon as you start cooking they come from all directions. They are Canada Jays" or "Gray Jays," but the most popular name is "Camp Robbers." They are very bold and will land right on the table if they see food.

Well, I took my pancake and sailed it through the air about twenty feet, and as soon as it hit the ground one of the birds was on it. He was soon joined by a couple more, and they had a tug-of-war with that pancake! They pecked it, pulled it, jerked it, but couldn't get it apart. They were very frustrated birds. It was too heavy to fly away with too! We rustled up something else for breakfast and when we left, they were still working on that pancake! I often wondered how that turned out.

It was about another fifty-five miles to Fort Nelson, which was established in the early 1800's as a fur trading post. It was named after an English Admiral. It was about three miles through town, wide and spread out. At Milepost 361, there is a good view of Indian Head Mountain. It is a high crag with a conformation resembling the classic Indian profile. Another mile or so is Teetering Rock. It's a large stone fragment visible on the skyline, left in balance by glaciers of the Ice Age.

At Milepost 375, the highway enters the North Canadian Rockies. Approximately Milepost 392 is Summit Lake, where the elevation is 4,218 feet above sea level. The Rocky Mountains are, of course, much higher, but this is the highest point on the Alaska Highway. Such wild beauty in these mountains! Such awesome scenery!

I think everyone should drive this highway at least once. If one ever does travel here, there are names of things and places you will never forget: Dawson Creek, Wonowon, Trutch Mountain, Pink Mountain, Steamboat, Lower Post, Watson Lake, Johnson's Crossing, Jakes Corner, Whitehorse (the capital city of the Yukon Territory), Haines Junction, Silver City, Kluane Lake, Destruction Bay, and Burwash Landing. Beaver Creek at Milepost 1202 of the

Alaska Highway is where the Yukon Canada customs office is located. It is another 20 miles to the Alaska border.

We made it! We were in Alaska. This was another highlight of my trip, crossing the border into Alaska. After stopping at the U.S. Border Customs Office, we proceeded on to Tok.

An interesting stop on the way to Tok was the Forty Mile Roadhouse at Milepost 1301.6. The Roadhouse was for sale in 1973 but I'm not sure if it is still open. When we were there, though, it was a very nice place. It had a full service gas station, a nice restaurant, nine small log cabins for rent to travelers, and also rooms for rent inside the Roadhouse. This is also the southern end of the Taylor Highway, which runs north from there 160 miles to Eagle, Alaska, on the south bank of the Yukon River.

The Yukon River runs a total of 2,300 miles from Atlin, British Columbia, and it enters Alaska near Eagle and runs 1,400 river miles across Alaska and empties into the Bering Sea. It truly is a mighty river. At Milepost 95 of the Taylor Highway, if you hold to the right, you cross the "Top of the World" Highway east to the Canada border. If you continue on east across the border, you come to the Yukon River, where there is a ferry to take you across the river, then it's just a short distance to Dawson City, and the Klondike gold fields where the "Gold Rush of 1898" took place.

At Milepost 66 of the Taylor Highway is the small town of Chicken, Alaska. This is also a gold mining area. It is said that there were a lot of Ptarmigan around there, so the folks who settled there were going to name their town after those birds. However, no one could spell "Ptarmigan" so they just named it "Chicken."

8 Tok, Alaska

Tok is a nice town several miles through and spread out. Right here, I'd like to pass on some important information. The pronunciation of two towns in Alaska: Tok and Valdez. Tok is pronounced with a long "O", and Valdez is pronounced with a long "E". Folks who have never been to Alaska have trouble with these two names. Betty and I did too, but it didn't take long to learn the correct way to say them — Alaskans were very helpful.

From there you can turn south on the Tok Cutoff and its 125 miles to Gakona Junction and the Richardson Highway. If you want to go to Fairbanks from Tok, just go straight through to the west. Dennis and I spent a couple of days there and we did meet up with Doug and Donna again. Unfortunately, things did not turn out for them the way they expected.

Upon arriving, they drove up to the church he was called to pastor, went up to the door and knocked. A man answered the door, but when Doug told him who he was the man said, "We don't need you anymore," and shut the door. You can imagine what a shock that was. They could hardly believe their ears. How could this have happened? They had just driven over four thousand miles only to be turned away with no explanation.

Dennis and I felt really bad for them, but we were at a loss for words. What could we say? What could anybody say, that might encourage them? Doug said that he had always wanted to see Alaska, and that was one reason he accepted the job that the church had offered him. He loved guns and hunting, and Alaska was certainly the place for that.

We all went over to the Tok Visitors Center to check it out. It was a beautiful building built of large round spruce logs. There were many displays of Alaskan wildlife, short videos to watch, and lots of other information. There we heard about a land offering called "Open-to-Entry." There were certain designated areas where land was offered, and they had maps showing their location. Any person of age 19 or older could file on five acres of land in one of these areas.

Each individual had to actually enter the land, stake out his five acres and go to the land office and get it recorded. Each corner had to be marked with a squared 4"x 4" post with the corner number on the post. You could only have a maximum of 400 feet frontage on any stream or lake. They told us an area 400 feet by 540 feet equaled five acres. The lease fee was $40 each year for five years.

When the five years were up, you could renew the lease for another five years at the same price. However, if, at the end of the ten-year period, you wanted to keep the land, you had to have it surveyed and make arrangements to pay for it. The land would be assessed at the fair market value at the time of entry.

These areas were quite remote and access to some of them was difficult, especially since break-up was just starting in Alaska and there was still a lot of snow. "Break-up" in Alaska simply means the transition from winter to spring. The rivers, creeks, and other ice and snow are "breaking up." Winter lasts from "Freeze-up" to "Break-up." You also hear the term "break-up boots" because when the ice and snow melt everything turns to mud for a while, so boots are a very necessary item.

When I found out you did not have to be an Alaskan resident to apply, I could hardly believe it, but did that ever stimulate my thought processes. I could get land in Alaska? Wow! It is very difficult to find the words to describe my feelings at that point. This seemed to be the answer to all my prayers and my dream of living in the wilderness. Doug and Donna were interested, and so was Dennis. We decided to go to Fairbanks to the Land Office and check this out further.

On our way we stopped at Dot Lake, Milepost 1361 on the Alaska Highway. It was a nice little place. The lodge building included a restaurant and post office; there was also a gas station and garage. These buildings were built in 1942 to accommodate the men who were building the Alaska Highway. After the highway was finished, the property was offered for sale to the highest bidder. It turned out that a man from Seattle, Washington got the property and soon moved with his wife and young daughter to Dot Lake.

Previously, this little lake didn't have a name. His wife Jackie was looking at the map one day and remarked that the lake was just a dot on the map. That did it. They decided to call their little community Dot Lake. A few years later, some Athabaskan Indians also made their homes there.

When we were there, they were in the process of building a new log building to replace the old lodge. A young native man named Jake and an older man were doing the work. Jake told us a story about three people, a woman and two men, who had come through the area the previous summer. He said they were from Florida, and they told him that they were going to live in the wilderness.

Approximately 18 miles to the northwest of Dot Lake is Dry Creek. He said that they went up Dry Creek a ways and set up camp. A few days later they came back through Dot Lake. Jake was quite surprised and asked them where they were going. They told him they were going back to Florida, and when he asked them what changed their minds, they just said "she can't cook". Jake laughed, and said he figured a bear had probably run them off.

Since Dry Creek was one of the open-to-entry areas, we decided to check it out. A few years before our arrival, they had built a new bridge over Dry Creek, and had built a temporary bypass road around the construction area. It was about 40 yards from the highway to the creek and it was a good place to park our vehicles off the highway. There was an old two-track trail leading south from there, so we took off.

We went about a quarter of a mile and came to an old pipeline right-of-way. We found out later it was a pipeline that was used to pump aviation gasoline from Haines Alaska all the way to Eielson Air Force Base 30 miles southeast of Fairbanks. It was an 8-inch pipe laying right on the ground. We didn't know at the time if it was still being used, but we looked around a little. Someone said, "Who wants land with a pipeline running through it?" So we left.

9 On to Fairbanks, Alaska

I must tell you that the Alaska Highway does not go all the way to Fairbanks. The first highway built in Alaska was the Richardson Highway. It was first known as the "Valdez Glacier Trail" in the late 1890's as the cry of "gold" echoed from the Klondike. It was later developed into the "Trans-Alaska Military Trail" of 1899. It has developed from "The Trail" to a major transportation artery into the Interior of Alaska. The Richardson Highway now runs from Valdez north to Fairbanks.

In the early days it was a long, hard trip by wagon and sleigh, through rain and mud, snow and cold. There were many roadhouses along the trail where passengers could get a hot meal and a warm bed. One such place was the Sullivan Roadhouse. It was located west of the present site of Delta Junction, across the Delta River. Two gold miners, John and Florence Sullivan, built it in 1905. The trail through this area went over some steep hills, and a few years later the Alaska Road Commission changed the route to avoid those places: the trail then by-passed the roadhouse by four and a half miles.

To keep their business going, the Sullivan's took their building down log by log, and moved it to the trail. They operated the roadhouse until 1922. After that it was mostly unused, except for an occasional traveler or trapper. Later, the military opened up a bombing range in the area. Surprisingly enough, the roadhouse survived the bombs, the harsh Alaskan weather, the occasional visitor, and forest fires, from 1922 until the mid-1990's, when it was again dismantled log by log, and moved to Delta Junction. There it was re-assembled and made into a museum. It has many of the original furnishings and artifacts from the early days. It is a very interesting place to visit, and it stands there today as a sort of monument to the rugged pioneers who came to, and settled this wild land.

Delta Junction is mile 266 Richardson Highway. Delta is also the end of the Alaska Highway, Mile 1422. For years there was a great controversy between the people of Delta Junction and the folks in Fairbanks about where the Alaska Highway ended, and I'm not sure if they have ever come to any kind of agreement on the matter, but the Alaska Highway does end at milepost 1422 in Delta Junction.

At the land office in Fairbanks they had a map of all the Open-to-Entry areas in the whole state. Peters Creek looked like a very remote area, and that's just what we were looking for. It was about 265 miles southwest of Fairbanks, and about 20 miles west of Talkeetna. Well, we weren't too smart at this point! If we had looked at the topographical map a little closer, we would have noticed that the actual boundary of the Open-to-Entry area at Dry Creek was about three quarters of a mile farther south from where we were. We could have saved ourselves a lot of trouble if we had taken the time to check it out better before running off to Peters Creek!

During all of this I'd been thinking that if this worked out for Betty and me, and we really did get some land, five acres might not be enough. I could only file on five acres myself. We would have to get all of our firewood from it, and I didn't know how many, or what kind of trees would be on the land that we would get. We had decided that if we ever could move to Alaska it would be a lifelong thing, so I had to think ahead.

When we got to Fairbanks I called Betty. She, of course, had absolutely no idea about what was going on. I explained the Open-to-Entry program to her. She was surprised, because as far as either of us knew when I left Michigan, I was just on a sightseeing trip to Alaska. She told me that if things worked out, and we could get some land, that she would be willing to move to Alaska. All right!

I expressed my concerns that five acres might not be enough and explained why. I asked her if she would be willing to fly to Alaska, so we could stake out five acres for her too. She said she would be willing to do that. I told her that we had checked Dry Creek out, but it didn't look very favorable, so we were going to check the Peters Creek area about 20 miles west of Talkeetna and a hundred miles north of Anchorage.

47

On the Petersville road we met another couple, Billy and Rosie, who were from New York. They were just driving around looking for some property they could buy. They had not heard of the Open-to-Entry program, so we explained it to them. We told them that one of the open areas was near Peters Creek, and that we were on our way there to stake out land. They decided to go along.

This was the second week of May, and break-up was in full swing in Alaska. There were mud holes in the road that were impossible to get through. We had to cut small aspen trees and fill the mud holes so we could drive across. About 14 miles in, we came to Kroto Creek. We could see that the road coming down the hill on the other side was washed out so we parked our vehicles, got our gear together and started walking. We figured we had four or five miles to go to get to the Open-to-Entry area. On our travels along the Alaska Highway, my new-found friend Dennis told me that he was noticing all the old log cabins along the way, and thinking about what size cabin he would build if he ever got the chance.

On the side of the hill across Kroto Creek there was a small log cabin. As I mentioned before, Dennis was quite outgoing and as we approached the cabin, a man came out and was doing something in the yard. We were still a hundred yards away when Dennis saw him and hollered, "Hello there, my friend, do you mind if we come in and visit?" He said for us to come on in.

Just a few yards from the cabin door there was a black bear about half skinned out. He explained that he woke up in the night and the bear was looking in the window right by his bed. He reached under his pillow and pulled out his .44 magnum revolver and shot him right through the window!

When we got inside the cabin, Dennis stood there looking around and said, "Hey, how big is this shack anyway?" I don't remember what the man said, and then Dennis said, "I see you have an extra bed, do you have overnight guests sometimes?" I don't remember the answer to that one either. Doug nudged me and said that maybe we should get going. The man seemed a little agitated at all the questions, and we didn't want to end up like the bear!

We were optimistic about our plans. If we could get to Peters Creek and find some good land, we could get to Anchorage, pick Betty up, and get back and start staking. We could stake out her parcel while she was there and get her back to Anchorage in time to catch her flight back to Michigan. Then we could come back and finish staking out the rest of our land. Of course, none of us knew anything about Alaska, and we were in for some surprises.

We left the guy's cabin and started walking. There was still snow on the ground, but when we got to the top of the hill we discovered the snow was a lot deeper. Before long we were wading in snow over our knees. We walked until it was quite late and we were getting tired. We came to a large spruce tree where the snow had melted down some underneath it. We were able to set up our tents there and get some sleep.

We got up early the next morning, had a light breakfast, and coffee, and started out again. It was tough going—we walked until noon and still had several miles to go. We wondered if we would be able to stake out our land even if we made it to Peters Creek due to all the snow, and time was running out for us to get to Anchorage to pick Betty up. After a short discussion, we decided to forget Peters Creek; there was no way it was going to work. We were disappointed because it was a very remote area and that's what we wanted.

On the way to Anchorage we discussed our situation some more and decided that Dry Creek was our only chance at this point in time. We were late getting to the airport. In the 1950's Betty had lived in Anchorage and had worked for the Alaska Railroad as a secretary. She had several close friends back then, and wondered if some of them might still live in the area. She had no idea where we were, or when we would show up, so she looked in the phone book.

Sure enough, one of her former friends was listed there. She called them and they picked her up at the airport. She left a message at the ticket counter for us, and when we arrived we got the message and called her. Betty gave us directions to where she was, so we picked her up and headed north to Dry Creek.

There wasn't room for all of us in front so Betty and I crawled in the back and tried to get some sleep. Doug and Dennis took turns driving. It was about an eight-hour trip. I don't remember if we stopped in Tok or Dot Lake, but we all got some breakfast and relaxed for a while. None of us really got much sleep. Billy and

Rosie had gone to Fairbanks from Talkeetna and planned to meet us at Dry Creek in a day or so.

10 Staking the Land

We all got together and checked the map again. The map was drawn to a scale where one inch equals one mile, and there were no other measurements on the map. The distance from the Open-to-Entry boundary to the confluence of a little no-name creek that emptied into Dry Creek was one quarter-inch. We decided to stake our land on this no-name creek. It would later be known as the East Fork of Dry Creek.

Staking the Land

I had a 100-foot steel measuring tape and a compass. We took our 4"x 4" posts and a shovel and walked up the creek. When we got to the fork in the creek, we took the left fork. We measured 1,320 feet—which is a quarter of a mile—then, because there were no actual measurements on the map, we walked another fifty feet just to be sure we were inside the boundary. We put in one of our posts, and Betty painted #1 on it.

We measured 400 feet southeast along the high water mark of the creek and planted post #2. I used my compass to get the directions toward where the next post would be, and then we measured off 540 feet and planted post #3. I took a reading sort of northwest from there 400 feet and marked the spot. We then went back to post #1 and measured 540 feet and connected the two measurements for post #4. That was Betty's parcel. We worked a little longer, went out to our camp at the highway and had some supper.

Doug, Dennis and Billy at our camp at Dry Creek, May 1973

We spent the night at Dry Creek. Now we had to get her back to Anchorage. We stopped in Glenallen, on the Glenn Highway, to find a Notary Public to witness Betty's signature on her application for the land. We found one, and explained our need. Even though it was a Sunday, he said he would do it for us. We really appreciated his help.

That was just one of the many things that worked out for us. My meeting Dennis and Doug and Donna coming up the highway was another. Discovering that there was land available to non-residents of Alaska was *very* unexpected. Meeting Billy and Rosie on the Petersville road was another. Having all that help to get the land staked out and the fact that we couldn't get all the way to Peters Creek were two more. I believe God led us here to the Dry Creek area, in whom I was trusting for all of this. He certainly has been faithful to us, and I truly believe that this is the place He wanted us to have.

Well, we got back to the airport in time for Betty to catch her flight home. Now all we had to do was get back to Dry Creek and finish staking our land. We staked mine out next to Betty's, Rosie's next, then Billy's parcel. Doug and Donna decided to stake theirs on the other side of the creek. We staked out two five-acre parcels for them, and one parcel for Dennis. I want to mention that in the process of all of this, we did come across the campsite of those folks from Florida.

Jake was right! It sure looked like a bear had run them off. All the signs were that they had left in a hurry. There were pots and pans, dishes, silverware and clothes scattered all over. We found a pair of men's pants in the tent that had a couple dollars' worth of coins in the pockets. There was also a long rip in the side of the tent!

Our work on the East Fork was finished for this year. We went to Fairbanks and filed our applications at the Land Office. Billy and Rosie were heading back to New York, but told us they planned to be back in the spring of '74.

The two parcels that Betty and I staked are the best of all of them. We had a high and dry spot to build our cabin on and we have good soil for a garden, whereas the other parcels were very rocky. There are nice trees on all of the parcels, and the East Fork creek runs year round, and the water is good and cold.

An interesting note is that the Division of Lands decided to close the Open-to-Entry Program to non-residents after June 11, 1973, leaving it open only to Alaska residents. I don't really know, but my speculation is that they never anticipated such interest in the program from non-Alaskan residents. I don't know how others found out about the program, but there were literally hundreds of people from other states who came to Alaska and staked out land. We were unaware of it at the time, but fifty or more people had staked land farther upstream on Dry Creek.

The original plan was to allow people to have recreational cabins. I don't think that it was meant for people to live on the land permanently, year around, but there was nothing in the plan that prohibited it. We filed our applications on May 21st, 1973 so we just got in under the wire, so to speak. That fact was, to me, another sign that God was working this all out for our good. Right from the start I can see His hand in it all.

I want to tell you about a little experiment that Doug, Dennis and I tried out one day. We built a fire one evening to have coffee and some supper. During our conversation Doug mentioned he had noticed that the stems of the wild rhubarb plant were hollow. He wondered if a guy could get a campfire going again after it had been out for a while by taking a hollow stem and blowing into the ashes. There were still some rhubarb plants left from the previous summer.

Since we had planned on going to Fairbanks after we finished our supper, we decided to try it out. We had built the fire on mineral soil, with a ring of stones around it, so there was no danger of the fire spreading, and the air was calm. By the time we had finished eating, the flames had died down so we figured it would be safe to leave. We were gone about 18 hours. When we returned, Doug took the hollow stem, pushed it down into the ashes and started gently blowing. It worked! In just a few minutes he had the fire burning again. We thought that this knowledge might just come in handy someday. For that reason, I'm passing it on to you!

11 Back to Civilization

The next morning, we all headed south to Anchorage. While there, Doug and Donna met up with some folks who had a dog they wanted to give away. It was an Alaskan Husky, part Siberian, and had blue eyes. Doug and Donna really liked the dog, and would give him a good home. Doug said that when their little boy, Jimmy, saw the dog he said, "nook." That sounded like a good Alaskan name, so that's what they named him. I wondered to myself how "Nook" would get along in the hot climate of South Carolina, but he did just fine.

Well, Dennis was going to spend some time with his friends in Anchorage, and Doug and Donna were going to spend some more time there also, but it was time for me to head back to Michigan. I drove back up to Dry Creek and spent one more night there. This was quite an emotional time for me! The only way I can explain my feelings is to say that for the first time in my whole life, I felt like I had found the place where I was supposed to be. I felt like I was truly "home," and I did not want to leave.

I stopped at Tok the next morning and called Betty. She was glad to hear that we had gotten everything done, and that I was on my way home. She also told me that Ed, Eileen and Amy had left Michigan and were in Canada somewhere around Dawson Creek. We had talked about meeting somewhere along the way. If they were in Dawson Creek we would have about the same distance to go to Watson Lake, in the Yukon Territory. Betty was our liaison. Ed and Eileen got there a day before I did, but they waited for me and we had a nice evening together.

We saw the famous "Watson Lake Signposts" where many people who came through put their names, where they were from, and — if they knew — how many miles it was from Watson Lake to their homes. It was quite impressive.

Famous signposts at Watson Lake, Yukon Territory 1973

We hated to say "goodbye" in the morning, but I had about 2,500 miles to go yet, and they were anxious to get to Alaska. Despite the long road trip, Amy was having fun. Eileen told me that a relative had made up some fun things for Amy to do; something different for each day to keep her occupied. That was surely a good idea and I'm sure it helped a lot, but I still wonder how many times they heard a little voice from the back seat, "Are we there yet?"

Sourdough breakfast before we said our goodbyes

My truck engine had been making a ticking noise for a while. I was between Grande Prairie and Valleyview, Alberta, Canada, when the engine began to miss on one cylinder. I got into

Valleyview ok and stopped at a garage. I explained to the mechanic that the engine was missing on one cylinder, and he asked me to start it up. He listened to it and gave me the sign to shut it off. He suggested that I go next door to the café and relax and he would see what he could do about my truck. That sounded like a good idea so I went over and got a cup of coffee and a sandwich.

About an hour later the mechanic came in and told me my truck was ready to go. I guess I looked a little surprised that he had fixed it so quickly. He explained that there was a truck just like mine that had been wrecked a while back. He knew what the problem with my truck was—an exhaust valve had broken. So he went over to the junkyard, took that other truck's engine apart and got the part he needed. Then he came back and installed the exhaust valve in my engine.

I don't remember what he charged me, but I remember thinking at the time that it was very reasonable. I want to say here that all of the people I encountered in Canada were very nice people. They were very friendly and accommodating folks!

That was the only problem I had with my truck on the whole trip. The rest of my trip home was relatively uneventful. All went well, and I arrived home to return to work on June 1st. Betty and I started making plans to move to Alaska. We were both going to work another year to get all of our bills paid, purchase any equipment we would need to build our cabin, and start living in our wilderness home.

12 Getting Ready to Roll

We spent as much time out in the woods as we could during the summer and fall of 1973. We roasted hot dogs and talked about Alaska. What would it be like, living out in the woods? How large of a log cabin would we build? We bought books about living in the wilderness and books about the edible plants and berries that could be found in Alaska. We read that rose hips are loaded with Vitamin C, a very necessary part of the daily diet. We wondered if there were rose hips in Alaska.

In the winter of 1974 I spoke with my employer about my trip to Alaska. I explained that when I started my trip it was just for sightseeing. Then, after I got to Alaska I found out that I could get some land. I told him how all my life I'd wanted to live out in the wilderness, and I felt that this was my chance to make that dream come true. I told him that I planned to quit my job and move to Alaska in May. He was very understanding, said it was okay and that he hoped it would all work out for me. Betty also spoke to her employer and, except for thinking she had suddenly gone stark raving mad, they wished her well.

My co-workers were mostly supportive. Some said that they would sure like to do something like that, but they knew they could never talk their wives into it. One of them said, "You'll be back, Bob," and I said, "No, I may come back for a visit someday, but I don't plan to live here again."

Okay! The word was out and we could concentrate on our move! I had a two-wheeled trailer with a four foot by eight-foot bed and 16 inch sides. I built side racks four feet high all around. I built a gable type roof and after we got it loaded, I covered the whole thing with a tarp to make it as weatherproof and dustproof as possible.

I want to tell you a humorous story that happened while I was building this trailer. A small neighbor boy from across the street came over and asked me what I was doing, so I told him I was building a trailer. I asked him what his name was and he rattled off his whole name, quick as a wink—a really sharp little guy. I'd guess he was five or maybe six years old.

I was getting ready to use my power saw and told him he'd better get back out of the way or I might cut him with the saw—meaning, of course, that I might accidentally cut him. He came right up close to me, stuck out his chin, looked me right in the eye and said, "You do and I'll tell your mother!" It was all I could do to keep from bursting out laughing. He turned around and went back across the street to his house. We've had a lot of laughs over that one. After all these years, I still have to chuckle when I think of it.

We already had a snow machine and we would take that along. We also bought a small travel trailer to tow behind Betty's car. I had a Citizens Band (CB) radio in my truck, and I installed one in Betty's car so we could communicate while driving. They came in very handy on our trip to Alaska. I had one more thing to take care of before we left Michigan.

In early January of 1974, I had injured my back. We were working at the plywood factory in Gaylord. The sawing operations in the factory produced a lot of fine sawdust, which resulted in frequent fires. Some of the roof joists were badly burned and weakened, and had to be replaced. They were 4 inches x 12 inches x 20 feet long and were heavy. We had to remove the "built up" roof system of tar, paper, and plywood to get at the joists. We tied a rope around each end of a joist and lifted it out of its socket, walked along the opening to solid roof and stacked them for later removal.

On one of them, the guy on the other end jerked his end out before I was ready. My end came out of its socket and was on its way down. I had to grab my rope hard to stop its fall and when I did, I heard a snap and my back really hurt. There were workers down below, so I couldn't let that joist fall. I had several visits with a chiropractor that winter, but my back wasn't getting any better so I told him that I thought we needed to do something different. He made an appointment for me with a specialist in Traverse City.

The first thing the specialist did was to put me on his table and measure my legs. He found that my right leg was ½ inch shorter that my left leg. He explained that because of the difference in the length of my legs, when I grabbed the rope and put the pressure on my back, instead of the pressure pulling straight down it slipped sideways, tearing ligaments and muscles. His solution to the problem was to prescribe a half-inch lift on the heel of my right shoe. It worked! The pain was gone. He made another appointment for me around the middle of April.

When I went for my appointment I told him that the lift on my shoe worked. I also mentioned that we had gotten some land in Alaska, and were planning to move in May. I told him that I was going to build a log cabin on it, and we were going to live a wilderness lifestyle.

He looked at me for a moment and said "Well, Bob, I'm not going to try to talk you out of doing that, but your back has been seriously damaged, and I think that if you try to do a lot of heavy lifting you're going to make it worse." We talked some more, and he told me that if I was determined to do this, he would have a brace made up for me to wear anytime I would be lifting or doing heavy work. I promised him that I would wear it and he said he would call me when the brace was ready.

When he called, I drove to Traverse City and got my brace. It was made of a very strong fabric. It had two flat steel bars that were positioned on each side of my backbone and bent in, in the lower back area to support my back when bending and lifting. It covered my body from just under my arms to my waist and it laced up the front. I did wear it whenever I was doing heavy work. On warm days it was miserable, but I got along just fine and my back is in good shape today.

13 Second Thoughts? Never!

In retrospect, I can understand why folks thought we were a little crazy. We were leaving the relative safety and security of civilization, our families and friends, to go close to 4,000 miles, build a log cabin in the woods, and live there for the rest of our lives? Hmmm!

My son Rob, his wife Kitty and their little daughter Candy, Betty's parents and grandmother, her two brothers and their wives and an aunt were still living in Michigan. Of course we did not know when or how long it would be before — or even if — we would ever see them again.

 Russ used to say that he was marching to a different drummer than most folks and that's the way I felt about myself too. I kept my nose to the wind, so to speak, and the wind was coming out of the Northwest. I could neither turn to the left nor to the right, but had to push on straight ahead.

For the most part, the kids were okay with our planned move, especially Brian. That may just have been because he was a boy. This kind of thing is just naturally more interesting for boys than for girls. Pam seemed sort of on the neutral side, but she was a quiet girl anyway.

It was different for Diana. She was a very outgoing girl. She had lots of friends, was 1st chair flute in the school band, and when she finished high school, she wanted to further her music studies. The Alaskan wilderness would not provide such opportunities. Even though we understood her position in all of this, we had no choice but to bring her with us. We knew that they would be doing home schooling in Alaska. I told her that after she graduated from high school, I would do all I could to help her to continue her education.

During the summer and fall of '73 and the winter of '74 we went to garage sales, flea markets, and secondhand shops looking for things we would need in the wilderness. We bought a treadle sewing machine, a wood burning stove and stove pipe. I bought a "one man" and a "two man" crosscut saws, axes, an adz for flattening round poles for floor joists, and tools for working the garden.

I also found what is called a 'pick-a-roon'. It is a steel hook with an axe handle that you can stick in a log to roll or move it, or to pick up a piece of firewood. I found it to be a very useful tool. I bought two cant hooks for rolling logs, a four-foot and a six foot one. I also bought a chainsaw. I really wanted to build my cabin the old fashioned way with hand tools, but I also realized that it would be slower and I might have to resort to more modern methods.

We bought two large crocks. They were about 18 inches in diameter and about 30 inches high. We planned to use one to make sauerkraut, and one for preserving meat for summer use because we would have no way to keep it cool.

I planned to use a method that my stepdad told me about. He was born in the late 1800's and raised on a farm in the early 1900's. They didn't have freezers so they had to figure out a way to keep meat from spoiling. That's where the crock came in. They would sear the pieces of meat in a hot frying pan on both sides, put a layer of meat in the bottom of the crock, packed tightly; then pour melted fat over the meat to seal it off so air couldn't get to it. They continued this process, a layer of meat covered with the melted fat until the crock was within an inch or so from the top and then pouring more fat on it to seal it. He said that this process worked very well, and they could keep meat all summer.

We packed the pickup and trailer with the things we would not need during the trip, and put everything else in the travel trailer. We spent a busy two weeks getting all of this done, but the day finally came when we had everything packed up and we were ready to start our trip to Alaska.

14 On The Road

We all slept in our sleeping bags that night. By the time we were up and ready to go it was late morning. We loaded up the rest of our stuff and got on our way. Finally! We were northbound on Interstate 75!

I think we were all in a state of euphoria, at least I was. Heading off into the "unknown," well, sort of, but the feeling of adventure and anticipation was almost overwhelming. Even though I had traveled that same route the year before, it was still exciting. Betty drove the car with Diana and Pam riding with her, and Brian rode with me. I want to mention here that Betty had never pulled a trailer before in her whole life, so this was something really different for her.

If one has never pulled a trailer before, there are a few things you need to know. For one thing, you need to be aware of the fact that it takes a lot more distance to pass another vehicle, so you have to allow yourself a lot more room. The way I like to do it is to travel at a safe speed, a little below the speed limit, and let the other drivers do the passing. Betty was a little apprehensive at first, but we drove slowly for a ways until she got used to it all, and she did very well.

When we stopped for the night, we had to unload the travel trailer to make room for Betty and the girls to sleep, and in the morning we loaded it all up again. Brian and I rolled out our sleeping bags in the car seats. This was not the best of sleeping accommodations, but it would work for us for the next couple of weeks.

I think it may be different now in Canada, but in those days a person could just pull off into a gravel pit and camp for the night. It sure helped on traveling expenses. We enjoyed viewing the scenery and eating in a different restaurant whenever we stopped.

As we were getting close to Edmonton, Alberta, Canada, I pulled off the road to check my map. The road atlas we had was not very detailed, but I was looking to see if there was a bypass road around the downtown area. I saw what looked like a bypass so we went on. Well, either there was no bypass road, or I missed it.

We found ourselves in downtown Edmonton during rush hour. Not good! At one time we were going the wrong way on a one-way street—also not good! Somehow we finally found our way out of that nightmare, and were again headed west. I think it was a miracle that we didn't have an accident—what problems that would have caused us. We thanked God that we got through it without a scratch.

Before long we were approaching Dawson Creek, British Columbia. Of course, Betty and the kids had never seen Milepost "0" of the Alaska Highway, so that was interesting for them. We decided to stop for the day a little earlier than usual. I unhitched the travel trailer from the car and we took a ride around the area to see the sights. We had a nice supper and relaxed until bedtime.

Things went quite smoothly. Our vehicles were running well, the weather was nice and we were enjoying our trip. We stopped at Muncho Lake for a break. It has beautiful dark, blue-green water due to copper deposits under the lake. Watson Lake was a nice little town and we also stopped at Whitehorse, Yukon Territory. There was a very nice museum there and lots of other sights. There was an old sternwheeler docked there that used to run up and down the Yukon River.

At about Milepost 1,053 we came to Silver City, also called Kluane. This is a ghost town. There were very old buildings in various stages of falling apart, old 55-gallon drums, old machinery, and parts of the same laying around. It was interesting to speculate about the people who had lived there, what were they like, and what life was like in the days when it probably was a busy little town.

After leaving Silver City, we crossed Slim's River Bridge, which was at the head of 35-mile long Kluane Lake. Just across the bridge on the left is Sheep Mountain. The white Dall sheep can often be seen on the grassy slopes of the mountain.

The Citizens Band radios that I had installed in our vehicles came in very handy. Sometimes it seemed to make the time go faster as we would comment on the beautiful scenery, what we did yesterday, or what tomorrow might be like. They were also very handy to keep track of other traffic.

One such time was when we were coming around Sheep Mountain. Betty was traveling a half-mile or so behind me. She came on the radio and said that there was a big semi-truck coming up behind me, and he was driving very fast. I could not yet see him in my mirrors because the road was curving around the mountain. I was concerned because we could not see very far ahead due to the curve. He was coming very fast; also, I saw a large rock ahead of me on the left side. It looked to be 12" to 16" in diameter. As the truck passed me, his right front wheel hit that rock and scooted it over right in front of me.

Well, there was nothing I could do but go straight ahead — the truck was very close on my left, and the ditch was very close on my right. The truck bumped along over the rock and the trailer bumped over the rock. Of course the big truck kept going, but I stopped to see if there was any damage to my rig. We hit that rock hard, but there was no damage. Once again, we thanked God for his protection. That was the first close call we had, but it would not be the last.

It was a little over 150 miles from Kluane Lake to the Alaska border. I don't remember exactly where the next incident happened, but there was a long steep hill down, and right at the bottom of it I discovered I had a flat tire on my trailer. I pulled over as far as I could and stopped. I mentioned earlier that the Alaska Highway was very narrow and there were no shoulders. From where we were the road started a long, steep ascent. It was obvious if traffic came down both hills with me at the bottom fixing my flat tire, things could get very complicated in a hurry.

I sent Diana back up to the top of the hill we had just come down to warn drivers of the danger below, and Betty drove on up the hill ahead to do the same for traffic coming from the other direction. The flat tire was on the left side so Brian and I were working right in the middle of the road. We had just gotten the wheel off the trailer when I heard a big truck coming down the hill, and he was really moving. I told Brian to "hit the ditch." That driver didn't slow down a bit and roared past. Thankfully, there was no traffic coming from the other way.

We thanked God again for keeping us safe. I'll mention here that I always had a lot of respect for long-haul truck drivers, but I lost a lot of that respect on our trip to Alaska. That was one reason for it. When we got to Tok, Diana spotted that truck at a truck stop, and she wanted to go in and tell him off for not heeding her warning. She said he had to have seen her trying to flag him down, but he never slowed down a bit. Well, we decided that wasn't a good idea so we kept on going.

On May 30th, 1974 we crossed the border into Alaska—what a great feeling that was! We had some friends who had moved from our area in Michigan to Juneau, Alaska. When Eileen, Ed and Amy arrived at Haines Junction the year before, they turned south on the Haines Highway to Haines, Alaska, then took the ferry to Juneau. They wanted to check Juneau out. I don't remember how long they stayed there, but after a while decided to go on to Fairbanks. They liked Fairbanks and stayed. So we went on up to Fairbanks and spent a few days with them.

Checking the Rigs

Bob and family with Amy at Ed and Eileen's in Fairbanks, June 1974

The truck and trailer upon arrival in Fairbanks

15 Starting our Cabin

We returned to Dry Creek on June 5th, 1974 to start building our cabin. Needless to say, we were excited. My dream was really beginning to take shape, and by now it was Betty's dream too. We set up camp where I had camped a year earlier. Betty and the girls slept in the travel trailer and Brian and I slept in a tent. Every morning after breakfast we would each carry what we could and head for our property.

There was an old trail along the bank of the creek that we used. It was grown over in places with brush, but we gradually got it cleared so it was easier walking. I mentioned before that when we were reading our books about Alaska we wondered if there were any rose hips in Alaska. There was a place on our trail that we named "rose hip ridge." The rose bushes were about five feet high, and for a distance of about a hundred yards, all you could see was wild roses. In fact, there are wild roses all over this country, so getting enough Vitamin C is not a problem.

We walked in the creek bed whenever the creek was dry. Usually the main branch of Dry Creek was dry, unless it rained a lot. In the summer of '74 it did rain a lot, especially in June. I think it rained every day, at least part of the day. Some days it would be raining when we woke up and rain until noon. We would get soaking wet walking through the tall grass, work for 4 or 5 hours and walk back out to have supper. We didn't really get a whole a lot of work done those days.

It was just a mile back to our property, as we found out nine years later when we were able to get a road in all the way to our cabin. But we were carrying building supplies and tools so sometimes it seemed a lot farther than a mile. We did have a couple of resting places along the way, however! We were all out of shape physically when it came to this type of activity, but by the end of the summer we were in pretty good condition. I lost 40 pounds that summer.

After a few trips we got the tools we needed back to our cabin site and we finally got started. There were a lot of big, tall spruce trees on the property. I decided to build the cabin 20 feet by 24 feet. The logs were long enough so that we didn't have to do any splicing between corners. The logs tapered quite a bit, from 8" or 10" on the large end down to 4" to 6" on the small end at 28 feet.

The first thing we had to do was cut the trees and brush out of the area we had chosen to build our cabin. After that was accomplished, I set up some batter boards at the corners. I measured the size of our cabin on the batter boards and drove a nail in at those points. Then I pulled a nylon line around the nails, and squared it up.

Bringing in a big one!

I dug holes about 16 inches in diameter and 24 inches deep at the corners and every 8 feet in between. The kids carried stones from the creek to fill the holes, and then we found some large flat stones for the top to lay the logs on. I cut the first cabin log down with my axe, just for the heck of it. However, I used my chainsaw after that. We heard that snow comes here in October, and sometimes September. I didn't know how long it would take to build our cabin, so I decided that I'd better get it done as soon as I could, and do it the fastest and easiest way.

It turned out that Betty and Pam were the main log peelers, and Diana and Brian worked with me, but sometimes we helped peel too. I'd cut down two or three big trees a day, cut the limbs off, and then we all pitched in and worked at peeling them. The side logs were 28 feet long and the end logs were 24 feet long. I had a four-foot overhang on each end of the cabin so the roof framing logs were 32 feet long.

The first side logs were flattened where they rested on the foundation stones, then the end logs were notched to fit on top of them. An important thing to remember when building a log cabin with round logs is to notch the bottom of the logs, not the top. This method prevents any water that might get on the walls from laying in the notches and rotting the logs out. Many of the old log cabins that I have seen were built by notching the top of the logs and have been destroyed by water laying in the notches. I believe that a properly built log cabin with a good roof will survive for hundreds of years.

Trees in Alaska taper a lot so we had to reverse them to bring the walls up level. We cut strips of insulation about 4 inches wide to lay on top of the lower log before rolling the next one in place. That sealed the gap between the logs very well. We cut small trees 4 to 5 inches in diameter and 26 feet long for the floor joists—an extra 6 feet on the west side for a porch. We put a 10-inch log in the center of the cabin to support the floor joists. After they were in place, I flattened them to make a place for fastening the plywood so the floor would be level. We laid the joists on the first round of side logs and continued up with the walls.

Getting a big one up on the wall

Since the logs were long enough to build the cabin without any splicing, I decided to cut the door and window openings out after the walls were up. I bought some 3/8-inch x 12-inch spikes and drove them into the logs about every 4 feet, and 8 inches from where the window and door openings would be. I bored a hole an inch and a half deep and drove the spikes there, to allow for shrinkage and settling of the logs.

I cut some 4 foot pieces of small logs about 4 inches in diameter and we laid them down as skids to pull the logs over. We tied two ropes around the end of the logs—one for Diana and one for me. Brian kept placing the skids under the logs as we went along. We only had to drag them about a hundred yards for the farthest ones, and of course some were closer. They were very heavy and dragged hard.

Notice how the tapered logs had to be alternated

One day we made a very pleasant discovery. We had two big logs ready to drag in. It had rained during the night, and when we started dragging the logs we found that it was much easier to drag them than before. The reason for that, we discovered, was that the rain on the freshly peeled logs made them slippery, just like they had been greased, so it took a lot less effort to drag them in. After that, if the logs were dry, we carried water from the creek and wet them down. A great discovery!

As I have already mentioned, it rained almost every day in June and we weren't getting much work done. By the time we got up in the morning, had breakfast and got back to the cabin site, it was somewhere around 10:00 am. We took a lunch with us, but we would leave around 4:00 or 5:00 o'clock to get back to camp for supper. On the days that it rained a lot we got even less work done. We had to do something different if we were going to get our cabin finished and ready to live in before winter. We had everything we owned parked out at the Alaska Highway and no place to live. We decided to move our camp back to the cabin site. We built a 16-foot square tent out of sheet plastic. That was a very good move.

Everyone waiting around for the beans to cook by our shelter

We would get up in the morning and the kids and I would get right to work while Betty made breakfast. When it was ready, we ate and then we all went back to work. We could work later also. We started to make more progress.

A very rare occasion for me: "building" some pancakes

16 We've Got Neighbors!

Well, the days went by and we kept working away on our cabin. It was good hard work, and in spite of being really tired at the end of the day, we were already enjoying our new home in the Alaskan Wilderness. Now I realize we were only a mile from the Alaska Highway, but it was 18 miles southeast to the little Village of Dot Lake, 65 miles southeast to Tok, 44 miles northwest to Delta Junction and approximately 150 miles northwest to Fairbanks. I think we could rightly say we were in the wilderness.

There were other people who had filed on land upstream on Dry Creek, and farther up from them were five more cabins. I was not happy with that because I had dreamed of having the whole valley to myself to hunt and trap. As it turned out they were all good neighbors and we got along just fine.

Shortly after we got started on our cabin Billy and Rosie from New York arrived on Dry Creek and started building their cabin. First, they built a small shed-style building out of 3-inch poles to live in, and then got started on their main cabin. It was a little smaller than ours for just the two of them. It was somewhere around 12 feet by 16 feet. It was really nice having them nearby. A lot of evenings we would go over to their place and sit by the campfire, talk and drink tea. It was a nice relaxing couple of hours after a long hard day.

One evening as we were getting into our sleeping bags, a shot rang out from their place. I decided I should go over to see if they needed any help. I walked over quietly to see what was going on. I couldn't see Billy, but Rosie was standing on a stump looking toward the creek. As I came up behind her, I guess I stepped on a stick or something; anyway she heard me and almost fell off the stump. Billy had shot at a black bear but she didn't know if he had hit it or not.

She said they had read a book about bears and that sometimes they would run off, circle around and come in behind you. When she heard me coming, she thought it was the bear. We all had a good laugh. Billy couldn't find the bear, or any sign that he had hit it, so he decided he missed it and they went back to bed.

One day, in the late afternoon, Rosie came over with some stew she had made and wanted us to try it out. It was very good, and it had meat in it too. I asked her what it was and she said it was squirrel. Well, I'll tell you, it was good! The squirrels here are like the little red squirrels we had in Michigan, and we wouldn't have ever even considered eating them. The only edible meat is the leg, but it was good.

Rosie really loved it out here in the wild, and she was so looking forward to living here. Sadly though, things don't always work out like you want them to. They got their cabin walls and the pole rafters up, and Billy decided he needed to go to Fairbanks. Something happened while they were there, and he decided that he didn't want to do this. He went back to New York and never came back to the creek to finish the cabin.

Rosie stayed a couple more months, but she couldn't do anything by herself so she went back too. They ended up getting divorced so that was the end of that. Doug and Donna also had problems, and they divorced and never came back to live, but Doug and his new wife have been back to visit a couple of times. Dennis got married, and his wife didn't want to live in the woods so Dennis didn't come back to build a cabin either. He has come back several times to visit though.

17 Cabin Rising

An interesting thing we discovered about working with logs is that they peeled real easy up until the middle of July. All we had to do was take an axe and get a strip of bark started, and we could pull long strips of it off. The sap quits running about that time of the year and the cambium layer dries up, so after that we had to use the drawknives to get the bark off. Drawknives are made of a sharpened steel blade with two handles that you pull towards you to peel the bark off the logs.

This must have been a Sunday. We're loafing!

We had all of our main cabin and roof framing logs peeled by then, so all that was left to do was cut and peel the smaller poles that would make up the roof. There were many small spruce trees around 5" in diameter so we used them. They all had to be draw-knifed. Pam was our "champion peeler." Every morning Brian and I went out and cut 15 or so trees, and Pam peeled them. She worked hard and really stuck with the job. She wore those yellow fuzzy work gloves. They got so full of spruce pitch that when she took them off at night, they would stand up all by themselves. She got a big laugh out of that.

Well we all worked very hard that summer. It has been said that, "All work and no play, makes Jack a dull boy." I believe there is some truth to that. We worked six days and took one day off to relax. There was a little chapel by Dot Lake, and we would usually go to church on Sunday mornings, then go over to the restaurant afterwards and have a hamburger or something.

Sometimes the pastor and his wife would invite us to dinner with them and we would stay for the evening meeting and then come back to camp. As the days grew shorter it would be quite dark by the time we got back to our parking place at the highway, and we would have to walk to our camp in the dark. That was okay, but sometimes we forgot to take our flashlights with us. There were times though, even if we had our flashlights that as we walked along, suddenly the goose pimples would pop out all over. We didn't see or hear anything; it was very strange. I don't know if there was a bear or other danger around, but the experience made me wonder if humans have a sixth sense like some animals do. Anyway, we had no explanation for it.

Ed and Eileen had spent a year in Alaska before we arrived. One day Ed mentioned that one thing he liked about Alaska is that when winter comes, it stays. Not like Michigan winters, where we usually had a "January thaw." The temperature would get above freezing and make a lot of slush on the roads, and then freeze up at night, making driving miserable the next morning. Michigan also had frequent ice storms that made driving to and from work or any other activities treacherous. Ed told me that Alaska is not like that. Well, I liked the sound of that.

However, one morning in August, about the 23rd, we woke up to two inches of snow on the ground. My heart sank. I had the walls of the cabin up, and that day I was going to start on the gable ends and the framing for the roof. Now what will we do? How will we get the cabin finished if winter is here? Two days later it was all gone. What a relief.

Ed was right though. Sometimes at the beginning of winter, which could be as early as September, we will get a little snow, and it melts off. But generally speaking, it just gradually gets colder and the snow comes and stays and it doesn't melt until April, or sometimes even May.

We were now ready to start building the gable ends. Diana had not been feeling well for a few days, and wouldn't be able to help with that operation for a while. I wasn't sure how I was going to proceed without her help. Betty, Pam and Brian were not strong enough for that kind of work. Well, we just never know how things are going to work out.

The very next morning we heard someone yell, "Hello the camp!" It was our friend Dennis whom I had met on my trip to Alaska in 1973, and who had helped stake out our land. Dennis was a diesel mechanic and was on his way to Coldfoot, which was an oil pipeline camp located on the Dalton Highway about forty miles north of the Arctic Circle. He said he had a few extra days and stopped by to see if we would "let him" help us on the cabin. Yes, God works in mysterious ways. I told him of our situation and that he was an answer to prayer!

We were so thankful for Dennis!

I already had scaffolds built to work from. We had to figure out a way to get the plate logs, the purlins and the ridgepole up there. I want to explain what purlin logs are, in case some of you are not familiar with that part of a log cabin. The roof framing on a log cabin consists of the plate logs (they are the ones at the top of the side walls), the purlin logs, and the ridgepole. Of course, the ridge pole is the one at the very top of the roof, and the purlin logs are placed halfway between the plate logs and the ridge pole, to help support the rafters. Our cabin has only one purlin log on each side of the roof, which is all that was needed for the size cabin we built. On larger cabins, there can be two or more purlins, depending on the size of the cabin.

We cut two trees that were about 6 inches in diameter at the stump end and 30 feet long. Then we tied a rope to the small ends and leaned them against the cabin wall at about a 45-degree angle. We brought the big logs over one at a time, and tied them to the poles.

We pulled down on the ropes until the poles rested on the opposite wall, then we untied the ropes on the big logs, and rolled them over to the cabin wall. We set the plate logs in place on each side-wall, and built the gable ends up to where the purlin logs would set. We then brought the purlin logs up and set them in their places, and continued up with the gable ends until we reached the place where the ridgepole would go, and set it in place.

This was hard work. Those 5 logs, including the plate logs over the walls, were 32 feet long. They were green and they were heavy. While the rest of us were working at this, Pam was down there faithfully peeling the poles that would be the roof. We didn't have the money to buy lumber for the roof so we used these poles, laid side by side. It made a very strong roof. Dennis stayed long enough to help us get all the poles nailed down. If I remember correctly, there are 210 of those poles on our roof. That's a lot of peeling!

Roof framing complete

September 1974

As you can imagine, it took a lot of food to keep us going. Betty is a great cook and she did a superb job of feeding us. She also made what she called "fry bread." You have never tasted anything so delicious. She made up a dough — only she knows how she does it — rolls it out, cuts it about 3" in diameter and fries it in a frying pan. It rises as it bakes, and she gets it a nice golden brown on each side and it's ready to eat. She likes to say that her fry bread built the cabin. That's really true, it did. We sure put away a lot of it.

Betty making Birch Syrup

18 Our Wilderness Home

Because we had a lot of "stuff" and no place to put it, I built the roof with a 6-foot overhang at the sides. We put some poles down and stacked our boxes on them. While we were building the cabin we also got the idea to dig a root cellar beneath it. We hit permafrost about 2 feet down, but no problem. We just dug what we could, and a couple days later dug some more. It was about 5 feet by 6 feet, and 7 feet deep.

Finished Root Cellar

I lined it with small poles and plastic sheeting. As it turned out, that was a good idea. I also put in a 3-foot piece of 3-inch galvanized pipe from the root cellar to the outside for ventilation. It never froze in the winter, and in the summer the temperature stayed in the lower 40's. Perfect, no refrigeration needed.

OK! We had the cabin built, and the roof on, so I went to Delta Junction and bought some material to finish it all up so we could move in. We got 12 rolls of 90 lb. roll roofing, a roll of 6 mil plastic, fifteen 4'x 8' tongue and groove plywood ¾ inch thick, fifteen 1/2" x 4' x 8' Celotex, roofing nails, assorted spikes and other odds and ends. We also found some used windows that would work. We got lumber for door and window frames.

Cabin ready for roofing and bleaching the logs

We had to carry all of this the mile back to our property. I made some rope slings for carrying the plywood and Celotex. They had wooden handles and could be adjusted for length. By wrapping the rope around a sheet of plywood or Celotex, and holding the handle with one hand and reaching up and holding the top edge with the other we could carry them quite comfortably. Of course, we rested often. I carried the roll roofing in on a pack board.

After we got all of our stuff back to the cabin, I cut out the door and window openings. We put the Celotex down on the floor joists, and the plywood on that. I framed in an opening for the trap door to the root cellar and built a ladder for access to it.

I don't know if they even make Celotex any more. It was made of pressed wood fibers, and was used as insulation. I put it on the floor joists for that purpose, and it would also help keep moisture out of the floor and act as a cushion for the plywood. We then put in the window and doorframes. I built a 3-foot by 6-foot, 8-inch door of 2 x 6's. It was a very sturdy door, and would certainly keep any unwanted varmints out of our cabin—read bears!

We put the 6 mil plastic over the roof poles and the roll roofing over that. I put a coat of sealer on the plywood floor, and as soon as that was dry, we moved in. It was time–it was the 15th of October, and there was 2 inches of snow on the ground. As you can imagine, after a long hard summer, we all crashed for a few days and rested up.

I'd like to mention here that due to the logs being green and wet, they got a coat of dark green mold on the surface during the summer. No problem, we brushed a solution of water and bleach on them and they cleaned up really nice.

One thing I didn't think of, being as we were pilgrim wilderness dwellers, was the consequences of the relationship between green logs and heat. We got a good fire going in the wood stove, and in just a little while, it began to rain on us! The moisture from the logs condensed on the underside of the plastic on the roof, and dripped through between the roof poles. Oh well, live and learn! It was a small problem.

Note how nicely the logs cleaned up, November 1974

We were very happy and satisfied with our wilderness home, and we were not about to let that discourage us. Betty gave the kids some saran wrap to cover their schoolwork. They could see through it, and it kept their papers dry. After our first winter, the logs were dry and we didn't have that problem anymore.

Diana, Pam and Brian doing their schoolwork

19 Getting Settled

Our mailing address was Dot Lake, and we had to drive 36 miles round trip to get our mail. One day we were at the Dot Lake Lodge and the highway mailman came in. I asked him if I could put up a mailbox out at the highway so I wouldn't have to drive so far to get our mail. He said we could, so the next day I went to Delta and bought a mailbox.

We were still walking the creek trail and I wanted a more direct way to the mailbox. When I walked out to get the mail, I took a little different route each time until one day I came right out at the mailbox. The next day we all went out and I stationed the family along through the woods about 50 yards apart in as straight a line as we could manage. When we got lined out, I went back and blazed the trees. Then we spent a few days cutting trail. We cut it approximately six feet wide.

The trail was wide enough for the snow machine so we could haul our stuff in. This route would eventually be where our road came in. I made a sled out of spruce poles that I could pull with the snow machine. It worked fine. Of course, we had to leave our truck out by the highway.

Cutting the trail to the mailbox

So, how do you start a truck at 40 below? I had a propane "weed burner," which was just a large propane torch. I guess in some places they actually used them for burning weeds in late summer to keep the seeds from spreading. I took two sections of 6-inch stovepipe, put a 6-inch 90-degree elbow on it, and slid it under the truck so that it was directly under the oil pan. I lit the torch and put it in the end of the stovepipe. In just a short time the oil was warm enough so the truck would start. It all worked very well. One time, though, the oily gunk between the back of the oil pan and flywheel housing caught on fire. I was able to get my gloved fingers up in there and snuff the fire out. Exciting moments!

Well, we were enjoying our new life in the wilderness! One day someone suggested that we have a picnic. It was November 1974, and it was 40 degrees below "0". Why not? Betty mixed up some dough for "stick bread," got some other things together and we were ready. We learned about "stick bread" from our muzzle-loading friends. You make up bread dough and put it in a bag. When you're ready to eat, you take some and roll it in your hands until you have a roll about a half inch in diameter and six or eight inches long. You then wind that around a green stick and hold it over the fire to bake. It rises as it bakes. Keep turning it over the fire until it's a golden brown, and it's ready to eat. It's quick and easy, and delicious.

We all piled on the snow machine and sled and hit the trail. About ¾'s of a mile north of our cabin was an old pipeline right-of-way, but it was no longer in use. We turned east and soon came to an open place in the woods. We found some dry wood and got a big fire going.

I've heard that some Indian said, "White man build big fire, can't get near, Indian build small fire, get up close." Well, I think I can safely say he had never tried that at 40 below! While his "front" was "up close," his "backside" was freezing off!

We built a big fire, and just kept turning our bodies like a hot dog on a stick. The stick bread didn't work well. It was so cold that even if we did manage to get the dough wrapped around the stick, when we held it over the fire to bake, it just melted and fell off into the fire. It does work well in warm weather, though. We had fun anyway, and returned to our nice warm cabin in good shape and in good spirits. This was our first "wilderness" experience, but there would be more.

At this point I must digress for a moment, to tell you of a difference experience I've just had. A few years ago I put several Plexiglas windows in our outhouse. This morning, the larger window, about 16" square was covered with frost. The sun is now riding along just above the top of the plateau, and it was shining on that window. There are thousands of tiny frost crystals on that window and as I moved my head side to side, I noticed that each one of them reflected the different colors of the rainbow. What a beautiful sight. How did He do that?

This is just another example of God's amazing creation. When we lived in the city we never noticed a lot of the things that we have discovered living out here.

20 A Cheechako Goes Moose Hunting

A "Cheechako" is a person who is new to Alaska and its ways. When one has lived a year in Alaska he becomes a "Sourdough" which is a full-fledged Alaskan!

There was a special moose hunting season in this area during the first week of November, 1974. I would have liked to hunt, but the non-resident hunting license cost more than I wanted to spend, so I decided to wait until the next year to hunt. Ed came down to hunt though, so I got to go anyway. If he got a moose, I could help him with it. I was born and raised in "cold" country, but I learned a lot about real cold when I came to Alaska. It was 25 degrees below zero when we left the cabin.

Bob on the Plateau, November 1974

We walked up the creek about a half mile and up the side of the plateau eastward. We got to the top of the ridge, which ran southeastward, and walked slowly along. There was a light wind blowing and it was cold.

We walked until noon. We hadn't seen any moose, and we were cold and hungry, so we dropped down into a draw (a small ravine) out of the wind to have some lunch and get warm. I was carrying a metal match safe with a screw-on top.

There was only one problem—my hands were so cold that I couldn't grip my match safe tight enough to unscrew the cap. I was surprised; I couldn't believe it! I walked over to Ed, and asked him if he would open it for me. I'll never forget the look on his face! It was sort of a mixture of unbelief and a smile all in one. I told him that I wasn't joking; my hands were so cold and weak that I couldn't open it. I did feel a little ridiculous! Well, he obliged me and we got a good fire going and had our lunch and some hot coffee.

Now we were ready to get that moose. We continued along the ridge and soon spotted a bull moose down a draw several hundred yards away. We talked about how we would handle this situation. If we were hunting deer, one of us would stay put, and the other would circle around behind the deer and drive him up to the shooter. It worked for deer, it should work for this moose. Ed got situated. He was going to be the shooter since he was the one with the license. I took off.

Have you ever walked through the muskeg in Alaska? Well, I never had. Boy, did I learn about muskeg! Muskeg is made up of sphagnum moss, partially decayed vegetable matter, grassy tussocks and boggy ground. It can be knee deep, and is very difficult to walk in. It must have taken me an hour or more, to get down past the bull and start up the draw. I guess I didn't consider Ed's situation sitting up there waiting: I was sweating and he was freezing.

I started up the draw and as I went along, I expected to hear Ed shoot any minute. I was beginning to wonder what was going on, when the track I was following made a sharp turn, and went right straight up a hill—about a 45-degree slope. I couldn't believe the moose would do that instead of continuing on up to Ed. What a disappointment! When I got up to Ed, he was just about frozen. He had a small fire going, but it wasn't doing much good as far as keeping him warm.

All he could find to burn was small finger sized pieces of dried out roots. Needless to say, we hightailed it for the cabin. So much for our first moose hunt! In discussing the situation later, we considered several reasons why that bull went up the steep hill instead of up to Ed.

Halfway up Macomb Plateau—Johnson River in the distance, November 1974

One thing we didn't think about when I decided to "drive" the moose uphill to Ed is convection currents. In the late afternoon when the air is cooling, it flows downhill. Another was that he was getting Ed's scent as well as the smell of the smoke from his fire. I guess that maybe because it was so cold, our brains might have had a little frostbite and we weren't thinking so well. Anyway, we both survived and so did the moose — and it's fun to remember.

21 Necessity Calls

Up until this point, we had been busy getting settled in our new home and having some fun. It was good, but now I had to get down to more serious business, like getting a job of some kind. Our "bank" was getting low on funds.

When we came to Alaska, I knew that because of where we would be living, the only thing that would work is for me to get a job somewhere, work until we had enough money for a while, and then I could go back home.

I am a journeyman carpenter, and I intended to go to Fairbanks and join up with the guys at the carpenter's hall. We were at the Dot Lake Lodge one day in the early spring of 1975, and I mentioned to Ann—the owner—that I was looking for work. There was a man living in the area who worked for Columbia Mobile Homes in Fairbanks. Ann mentioned to him that I was looking for work, and he got me a job driving pilot car for them. He told me that it would be a short job because they would be making some changes in the way they operated. I told him that was o.k. and that I was thankful for the job.

We made trips to Haines and Anchorage, Alaska. I like to drive, so I was happy. I'm sure most folks know that trucking companies who haul large equipment are required to have pilot cars travel with them. They are usually pickup trucks with rotating beacons and warning signs and are very visible. They usually have one pilot car in front of, and one in back of the big trucks to warn oncoming drivers of the danger ahead. Some of the loads they haul are extra wide and take up the whole lane they're in, and sometimes they even extend into the opposite lane some, so these pilot cars are very necessary.

That job boosted our financial situation, but it wouldn't last long, so I decided to go to Fairbanks in July of 1975 and join the carpenter's union. They had a meeting every weekday morning.

Employers who wanted to hire carpenters notified the union officials, and carpenters who were looking for a job went to the union hall every morning. They called it "making call" to try to get a job. After a couple of weeks of making a call every morning, I got a job up at Prudhoe Bay on the North Slope. I would be working for Alaska General Contractors. I flew up to Deadhorse on July 25th, and I worked until the middle of December.

I was on the "C" or "third" list that non-residents were put on. Even though I had lived in Alaska more than a year, I was put on that list. The Carpenters Union also had a rule that those on the "C" list couldn't work past the end of the year. They also had a rule that when those on that list got laid off, they had to go back to the bottom of the list. Anyway, our "bank" was charged up again, and I was thankful for the job.

The food and living quarters were good. We worked seven ten-hour days. That was fine with me. As long as I had to be away from home, I might as well get in all the hours I could. I was laid off just before Christmas. Betty and the kids picked me up at the airport.

We had some money now, so we all went Christmas shopping. We got extra sets of warm clothing, and of course, more and better equipment for living in the woods. Very important items: Brian got a .22 caliber rifle, Betty got a .270 caliber Winchester, and I got a .300 Winchester magnum. I had a 30.06 rifle, but I needed something a little more powerful for hunting among the grizzly bears.

When we got home, the kids and I went out and got a nice Christmas tree. As you can see from the picture of the tree, spruce trees that grow in the wilds of Alaska are a little "skinny,", but it was our first one here so we thought it was beautiful!

Our first Christmas tree, 1974

Since I had been working up North during hunting season, I wasn't able to get our winter's supply of meat. A neighbor a few miles up the road told me that Alaska Fish and Game in Delta had some moose meat they had confiscated from an illegal kill and that if I went into Delta, they might give me some of it. A neighbor went in with me, and they were happy to give us the meat. The only condition was that we share it with our neighbors. Well, we certainly would do that. They gave us a whole moose, just lacking one hindquarter. We shared it with several neighbors, and we all had a very fine Christmas dinner.

Betty and the girls fixed a good dinner. We had moose steaks, potatoes and gravy, cranberry sauce—picked from the numerous local cranberry patches, vegetables, pies, and some of Betty's delicious "fry bread!" We invited some neighbors who lived over on Dry Creek, Billy and Judy, for dinner. Part way through dinner Billy quipped, "It sure is tough living in the frozen north!" We all got a good laugh out of that. Truly, we felt very blessed. Good food, good neighbors, and a wonderful God who provided for our needs then, and who still provides for our needs today. We are thankful.

22 Life on the East Fork

Two things that I wanted to do when I came to Alaska were to run a trapline and do some prospecting for gold. I guess everyone who comes here dreams of finding gold, and I was no exception. Billy and I were talking about these things one day, and decided to start a trapline. He had done some trapping before, and also was interested in prospecting for gold.

We started getting the things we would need. Traps, tie wire, wire cutters, small handsaws for cutting trails, and various other necessities. We already had snow machines. I bought a fold-a-sled for hauling our gear and for bringing back the fur we would catch. Might as well be optimistic! One of us would drive the snow machine and the other rode on the back of the sled. Neither of us was interested in using dogs. Some guys do, but as I always said, "When you shut the snow machine off, it stops eating!"

The only trails in this country are access trails to hunting and fishing places, so we had to cut our own trails wherever we wanted to go. The first couple of years we cut a lot of trail, and actually our trail cutting never ended because we were always looking for more trapping ground. We worked hard, but we enjoyed it. We were out in the fresh air and sunshine, and out where you could go almost any direction for a hundred miles and never see another man. Not that we ever would, but it was nice to know that we could.

It gets very cold here in the winter, so we set a limit of 25 to 30 degrees below zero for running the trapline. The winter of '74 – '75 was very cold. The last part of December and January we had a lot of days where the temperature was 60 degrees below. We had a thermometer that went to 60 below and it showed that same temperature for several weeks. I thought the thermometer was broken, but one day it started to rise.

Winter trip to Macomb Plateau in the early years

I walked out to get the mail one day at 60 below, just for the fun of it—a two mile round trip. When I got back to the cabin my facemask was solid ice and frozen to my beard. I had to stand by the stove for quite a while before I could get it off. It was exciting to write back to family and friends, "Wow, it's 60 below here!" However, after 40 years, it's not so exciting anymore.

One has to be very careful at those temperatures. Any skin that is exposed can freeze in just minutes. When we were out on the trapline Billy and I checked each other's faces often. If there were any white spots, that meant the skin was freezing and we needed to get it warm quick!

Besides schoolwork the kids had an ice skating area on the creek. When the weather is very cold, the creek freezes right down to the creek bed. The water backs up, and as the pressure builds, the water comes up between the ice and the creek bank and flows out on top of the ice. When that freezes it's as smooth as glass and makes for great skating. We would build a fire on the bank for them and they had a lot of fun.

Ice skating on the East Fork, 1975

Brian liked to fish and in the summertime he could catch small Dolly Varden in our creek. They were small, four to six inches, but he had a lot of fun with them. Once, he saw some of them and got so excited that he jumped in the creek clothes and all, and tried to catch them.

Our creek empties into the main branch of Dry Creek about a quarter mile downstream from our cabin. Dry Creek empties into the Johnson Slough, and the slough empties into the Tanana River.

Sometimes Arctic Grayling came from the Tanana right up into our creek too. There are also several small lakes not too far away that have some really nice Rainbow Trout. We fished those lakes both summer and winter and caught some very nice fish.

The kids warm up by a fire with dogs Wolf and Bear

East Fork of Dry Creek near our cabin

Details of Dry Creek
Johnson Slough
Tanana River

To The
YUKON RIVER

TANANA   River

RIVER

Johnson   Slough

BRIDGE

JOHNSON   DELTA JcT.
                 44 MILES
ALASKA
BRIDGE   Highway – Tok 65 MILES

NorTh

DRY   CREEK

EAST FORK

☐ ← Our Cabin

DRY CREEK To JOHNSON
SLough, JohNSoN SLough
To TANANA RIVER, TANANA
RIVER To YUKON RIVER,
YUKON RIVER To BERING SEA

104

A lot of hard work, but ready for winter. The scaffolding served as our 'cache' to keep animals out of our frozen food

Usually, we set aside the last week of March and the first week of April to get firewood. In February of 1975, Dennis and his friend Ray came for a visit and helped us get this nice pile of firewood. We used the snow machine and I built a wooden box for the sled to haul the wood in. We would run up and down the creek on the ice, looking for dry wood and windfalls. We hauled it back to the cabin and piled it up. We couldn't find enough wood on the creek so we got it wherever else we could find it. After a couple of years, I got tired of digging the firewood out of the snow, so I built a large woodshed. It held twelve cords of wood. I usually piled some extra outside, and we had enough wood for heating and cooking for a year. We all pitched in on that job and it was hard work, but we had fun too!

Hauling firewood

We tried to have fun together as a family whenever we could work it out. The correspondence school headquarters was located in Tok, and one of the supervisors made the rounds to the students in our area occasionally.

That was exciting for them because they could take some time from their schoolwork and visit with him. They also had special events from time to time and field trips. One time the school took them on a trip to the Southeast of Alaska. They also had fun projects they could do at home. On Sundays we went to church at the little chapel at Dot Lake. We usually went over to the lodge afterward and had hamburgers or something. That was a nice break too.

When we came to Alaska we still enjoyed our muzzle-loading activities, but we didn't join any clubs here. On the 4th of July we put our costumes on, shot my rifle, and threw the knife and tomahawk. I had gotten a section of tree trunk about 18 inches in diameter, put three legs on it, and used that to fasten the targets on. When Betty and the kids got so they could stick the tomahawk in the block consistently, we tied a string across the front of the target and had a contest to see who could cut the string first. It was a lot of fun. In later years hardly a family get-together in summer did not include throwing the tomahawk and shooting the Flintlocks.

I also put on a demonstration of shooting my flintlock rifle and tomahawk throwing at the Children's Home at Dot Lake one time. I enjoyed doing that, and they all enjoyed it too. Most of them had never seen anything like that.

Giving muzzle loading rifle demonstrations at Dot Lake

Close-up of the coonskin hat

One really nice feature of homeschooling the kids, was that we could be flexible. If we wanted to do something as a family, we could take a day or two and do it. They would work hard for a few days and get caught up in just a short time.

In the early spring of 1975, I decided to go black bear hunting. Did I think I was going alone? Yes. Not so! When I mentioned my plan, the whole family wanted to go. No problem, so we started packing.

I didn't know where any of the trails were in this country so we walked up the East Fork a ways and found a place that didn't look too bad for climbing. Well, it wasn't all that great. It was a rock field of loose stones, large and small, and it was quite difficult. One time Betty got up on a large flat rock and it started teetering and she thought she was going to end up back down in the creek. We finally got up to where the land rose up more gradually, and the going was easier.

We walked south until we came to a place where the land dropped off sharply down to the East Fork. It was at the head of a large valley with a small creek — an ideal camping place. We set up our tent, made a fire pit, and prepared ourselves for another "wilderness" experience.

Anyone who has ever camped out in a tent knows that a two-man tent is just large enough for one man. That's what we had, a two-man tent, but we had five bodies that would be sleeping in it. Talk about togetherness! I found a piece of rock about two inches thick, propped it up on some stones and built a fire underneath it. It really worked well. It took a while to get it hot enough, but Betty was actually able to bake some of her (by now, famous) fry bread on it.

The weather was nice—not too cold, lots of sunshine, and we were all enjoying our "camp out." We were high enough so that we could see for miles to the North and East. To the South and West were the high mountains of the Alaska Range. We didn't see any bears, but we enjoyed our time there. A few days later we had breakfast, packed up and headed down to our cabin.

Betty said that she didn't care how or where we got back down, but she was absolutely not going back down the way we came up! She sounded very determined about that! Well, we found another way down. It's a lot easier going downhill than it is uphill anyway. Here we were doing the things I'd only dreamed about. It was awesome!

The family in front of the cabin, 1975

Many evenings we had fun playing music. Diana played the flute and I played guitar. I also played the harmonica and accordion occasionally, and we would play and sing until we tired of it, and then play games or find something else to do. Those were good times. We miss those times now that the kids are all out on their own, but we still have the memories.

We've all had a lot of fun living out here where we could be free to pretty much live the way we wanted to live! However, there was lots of work to living here too. Betty was home schooling all three kids, and doing most of the cooking and cleaning. Of course, the girls helped as much as they could with the household chores, after their schoolwork was finished for the day. And some jobs required all of us to help out.

Somehow, though, during all of the work, Betty decided she wanted to try her hand at painting gold pans. I'm sure you have all seen them in souvenir shops and other places. I bought her several gold pans, and she went about picking out the colors of paint she wanted, she used real artists enamel paint, an assortment of brushes, and various other things she would need.

I'm not sure if she knew that she had talent for this sort of thing, but she soon showed that she did! She did some amazing work. She really enjoyed doing this! I can't remember how many pans she painted, but quite a few. She gave them away to family and close friends. Here are a few samples of her work:

Sketch of Bob by Betty

23 The Trapline

Billy and I were satisfied with our first winter of trapping. We cut a lot of trail, and brought home some nice furs. We have quite a variety of fur animals in our area. Marten are the most abundant, fox the next with four different color phases: red, black, silver and cross fox. We have wolves, lynx, coyotes, an occasional wolverine, muskrats, a few river otters in certain locations, and an occasional mink.

In the early years we had flying squirrels too. We never trapped for them, but caught one occasionally in a marten pole set. There are beaver also, but we weren't interested in them. The "profit versus work" ratio was pretty small so we didn't bother with them.

Wolverines, as I mentioned, were not plentiful, but we caught a few. They brought a good price. They are fierce and dangerous animals when they're caught in traps. They are not dangerous to humans when free and will keep their distance. No matter how cold it was, we have never found a wolverine or a lynx in a leg hold trap that was dead. They both have very thick fur and can survive very cold temperatures, even if they can't move around much. Wolverines rarely kill anything themselves, they live mostly on whatever some other animal has killed. I guess that's why they so readily come to a bait set.

I had an interesting experience with a wolverine once. I had a short line, about two miles long, that went from our cabin back to and along the base of the plateau. It was a surprisingly good producer for such a short line. I caught fox and lynx on it often, and occasionally a marten. This is where I caught the wolverine I just mentioned.

We had six to eight inches of fresh snow, and I needed to get out and re-do my ground sets. Note: ground sets are simply traps set on the ground, as opposed to a pole set for marten, or other type

114

of set up off the ground. When new snow comes one has to re-do the sets to keep them working. I only had a couple hours of daylight left, so I decided to check the short line. About a hundred yards before I got to my first set, I came across a trail some animal had made coming down the snow machine trail. It was made after we got the new snow.

It was difficult to tell what animal made it. When I got up to where my first set was, I discovered that some varmint had gotten into one of the two #4 traps I had there, chewed the drag pole in two, and left. From the signs I suspected it was a wolverine. They can't run too fast in deep snow with their relatively short legs, and this one had a trap on one leg, which would slow him down even more. I was sure I could catch up with it in a short time.

I kept looking ahead as I walked, and once I thought I heard a chain rattling. Sure enough, there he was, maybe 75 yards ahead of me. I could go pretty fast on my snowshoes and in a few minutes I caught up with him. I always carried a .22 caliber pistol with me on the trapline to dispatch small animals, if there was no other way to do it, and also my .44 magnum revolver for larger problems. When I caught up to him, he stopped and turned around to look at me.

I dispatched him with the .22. Well now, here was a mystery. He not only had my #4 trap on one front foot, he also had a #1 ½ marten trap on the other front foot. I call it a mystery because the closest marten set was four miles away on Sears Creek. There were no other trappers in the area, so where did he get the marten trap? I decided the next morning I would check my traps on Sears Creek.

About a half mile up Sears Creek, I discovered what had happened. A wolverine had climbed up the marten pole, gotten into the trap and chewed the pole off. Close by was a place where it had rolled around in the snow, apparently trying to get the trap off his foot. He couldn't get it off so he took off down the creek. He went down to the old pipeline right-of-way, turned west, and went in and out of the trees. He passed under a snare I had set for lynx, continued for about four miles, turned south towards the plateau, and got into the #4 trap! The mystery was solved.

Another time I caught a wolverine in a marten pole set on the same creek, only a couple hundred yards from where I caught the first one. It happened at least a day before I got there, maybe two.

He got in the trap, chewed about 2 ½ feet of the pole off, and took off dragging it. He only went a few yards, and the drag got hung up in some brush. He literally chewed off everything holding him and got away. Then he crossed the creek and got hung up again. He mowed the brush down and kept on going.

I didn't have my snowshoes that day. The snow was two feet deep, and it was tough going, but I figured that as long as he was dragging that piece of pole, he might get hung up again and I could catch up to him. Down the trail a short distance I found the drag. The wire holding the trap had broken; there was no way I was going to get him now. I always felt bad when I lost an animal. It happened very rarely, but it did happen. My first concern was not losing the trap or the fur, but what the consequences would be for the animal.

As for my gold prospecting plans, they didn't work out. Billy had done some prospecting in Arizona and other places, and knew what signs to look for as indicators of mineralization. There are many valuable metals in Alaska and each has its own indicators as to its presence in the rocky outcroppings and in the creeks. But we were mostly interested in gold.

When we were on the trapline, Billy was always looking for signs of mineralization. We discovered a basalt dike about six feet wide and three feet high that came down out of the hills and disappeared into the creek. Basalt is a dark, fine-grained igneous (related to volcanic activity) rock. He called it a contact fault, where two different types of rock meet. He told me that a contact fault is a possible indicator of mineralization, and that he thought it would be interesting to see what was in there. We staked out four claims.

We bought a case of dynamite and some steel rods to make chisels for drilling into the rock to make holes for the dynamite. We also got a 4" suction dredge for working in the creek itself in case we should find gold in the creek. We hauled all the stuff up on the snow machine sled, intending to come up the next summer and check it out.

As it turned out, Billy took a job in Fairbanks the next summer. I knew nothing about how to go about it, so we decided to put it off for another year. Well, due to an accident that happened, which I will explain later, we didn't get back up there until the second winter after that. Brian and I went up with the snow machine and sled and retrieved the suction dredge and all of the other stuff we had up there and brought it home. We never got back up there to check it out.

I mentioned that we had a case of dynamite up there. When we picked it up, it was really light. We discovered that something had gotten into it and had eaten, or at least carried off, all of the dynamite except four or five sticks. We had a lot of fun cogitating about that. There was some black hair around and we thought that it was either a black bear or a wolverine that had gotten into it. We imagined the animal jumping off a rock or creek bank and disappearing with a big bang!

24 Our First Caribou Hunt

In August of 1975, my half-brother Virgil and his wife Juanita moved to Alaska and settled in Dot Lake. He was a hunter too, so the following year we all decided to go caribou hunting. We have a resident herd on Macomb Plateau so that is where we would hunt. Caribou season opens on August 10th.

Our first Caribou Hunt, August 1976

We got our stuff together and started out the day before season opened. I still had not found out if there was an existing trail somewhere so we just went up where it looked like the easiest way. We definitely avoided the way we went in the spring of '75 though. The way we went this time wasn't much better, as it turned out. Before we got to where we wanted to go, Virgil and I were carrying the women's packs as well as our own. It was tough going, but we finally got there and set up camp.

It is really beautiful up there. The tundra was beginning to turn color. There were all shades of red, yellow, and different shades of green. I love that high country. Hunting up there is a real experience. It is a rolling terrain and you can see for two miles to the south and farther to the southeast. You can watch for hours and never see an animal, then suddenly, there they are just a few hundred yards away.

That's the way it was that first day of season. We got up early, had some breakfast and waited. A couple hours later, a herd of twenty or thirty caribou showed up about 200 yards away. I picked one out and shot—down he went. Then of course the herd turned around and disappeared to wherever they came from. We had a lot of day left, so Virgil and I skinned and cut it up, loaded it on our pack boards, and headed out. Betty and Juanita decided to stay and try to get one too.

First Caribou

There was a lumberyard and building supply in Delta that also had freezer lockers for rent. One time when we were in Delta we rented two of them, anticipating the possible need for them when hunting season came around. Virgil and I packed my caribou out, took it to Delta, and put it in the freezer. We went over to the Evergreen Restaurant, had some supper, and returned to the cabin. In those days we didn't have a road in to our property so that was an extra two miles that we had to walk every trip.

The pattern we set for this was that we would pack a load of meat out, take it to the freezer, have supper in town, spend the night in the cabin, and go back up to camp the next morning. I don't remember just how it happened, maybe we talked to another hunter, but we found the trail up the plateau. It was still a steep climb, but a whole lot better than the other ways we tried.

In checking it all out according to the topographical map, from the highway at roughly 1,400 feet elevation to our camp at 4,200 feet, we traveled six miles one way and gained an altitude of 2,800 feet vertically. That amounted to a little over 80 miles that we walked on that hunt. Even though it was hard work, we enjoyed it, and it would also prove to be a real benefit in another way, which I will get to a little later. We got up the next morning, had some breakfast, and headed back up to camp.

The weather had deteriorated, and it was foggy with a light rain. I didn't take my jacket with me because it was too hot to wear while packing meat out. I got wet and began to get really cold. I also became concerned about hypothermia. I always carried a black plastic bag with me for whatever I might need it for. I cut a hole in the bottom of it large enough to get my head through and pulled it down over me for a windbreak. It worked fine and I was nice and warm.

Up on top the fog was right down to the ground. As we were walking along the fog lifted, and about 50 yards in front of us there were 7 or 8 caribou. Virgil picked out a bull and dropped him in his tracks. We field dressed it and laid it up on a big rock so the four legged scavengers wouldn't get into it, and went on to the camp. I was quite sure that the women hadn't gotten any caribou, and I decided that when we got back to camp, I'd have a little fun. When we got there they were both sitting inside the tent out of the rain. I walked over and said "Ok, where are your caribou?" I was not expecting the answer I got. They both pointed and said, "Right over there." Was I surprised! They had both shot a caribou. That was great; we were very proud of them because neither of them had ever shot anything but targets before. The distance was only about 30 yards, but for two novices it was good shooting!

The Lady Hunters

Well, everyone had their work cut out for them. We were all excited and anxious to get back to the cabin, and have a big meal of caribou steaks! Later, they told us of their experience. They were both inside the tent out of the rain when the caribou showed up. Juanita said to Betty, "You shoot first!" And Betty said, "No, you shoot first!" After a few seconds of that, Juanita shot first, got her caribou; then Betty shot and got hers. It was hilarious to hear them tell about it.

We showed them how to skin and cut the caribou up, and Virgil and I went back and butchered his caribou and packed it out to the truck. We made several more trips packing out meat. The women stayed in the camp to take care of our meat and protect it from any varmints that might come along. The last trip they came back down with us. They had spent nine days up there. That was really something for two gals who had never done anything like that before.

Virgil and I got back from Delta and we planned to go back up the next day to pack our camp out. Diana told us she would like to go up and try to get a caribou. Pam and Brian also wanted to go, so we all took off. We stayed two more days, but she didn't get a chance to get one. In fact, we never even saw another caribou. She was disappointed.

Bob with some caribou and moose antlers early 80's

25 A Life Changing Experience

Well, we had a fun summer and a good hunt, but now it was time to get another job. I went to Fairbanks and started making call every morning at the carpenter's hall. Of course, I couldn't drive back and forth every day—it's a 300 mile round trip. The topper that I had built on my pickup came in very handy once again. I stayed in Fairbanks all week. I slept in my truck, went to a restroom in some gas station or restaurant to wash up in the morning, and went to the hall to see if I could get a job. No luck that week, so I came back home after call on Friday.

The kids were old enough to take care of themselves and our place, so the next week Betty went back to Fairbanks with me. She was able to get a job and that helped a lot. We would go home on the weekends, and go back in time for me to make call on Monday morning and for her to get to her job. As I mentioned earlier, even though I had worked out of the hall the previous year, when I got laid off in December of 1975, I had to go back to the bottom of the "C" list. That meant that everyone ahead of me on the list got called before I could get a job.

We lived in the truck for about a month and a half. We went home on weekends and back to town early Monday mornings. The weather was getting cold and it was pretty miserable. The temperatures were getting down to ten below zero at night so we had to do something different.

One day we were looking at a bulletin board—I think it was up at the University—and we saw where a guy would trade a room in his basement for some carpentry work he wanted done. We went to see him and made an arrangement with him. So we had a nice warm room to sleep in, and I did some work for him. Their names were Richard and Sally, and they had a little baby boy. They were nice folks, and we got along very well.

We were there a couple of weeks, and I finally got called out for a job. I had a choice to make. I could go back to Prudhoe Bay, or I could go to a place west of Prudhoe and south of Barrow called "Camp Lonely." I decided that since I'd already been to Prudhoe Bay, I'd go to Camp Lonely. That was the 11th of December 1976. We came back home and I got my stuff together. Betty drove me to Fairbanks the next day, and they flew me to the airport at Deadhorse and on to Camp Lonely the same day.

The next day an apprentice carpenter named Mike and I started trimming out a metal building. It was 18 feet to the eaves of the building, and we were putting the corner trim on. We could get the first 12-foot piece on working from a ladder but it was difficult. The temperature was 50 degrees below zero and there was a stiff wind blowing. If we let go of the ladder the wind blew it over.

We got through that day ok, but the next day I asked the foreman if we could use the crane that sat nearby. He told me that the operator had sat in the crane all day the day before and no one used it, so they sent him out on a "cat train." There were other work sites in the area that needed supplies and workers periodically, so they sent the stuff out with bulldozers pulling sleds called cat trains.

The foreman said he would try to find another operator. A short time later he came back and said he had found an operator, but he was someone that he didn't know; so to check him out. The man lift, or cage, as I called it, was sitting about 50 feet away so I asked him to pick it up and move it over to the corner of the building where we were working. He swung over and picked it up and set it down right where I wanted it. Everything seemed ok so we loaded up our tools and climbed in. This cage was about 3 feet by 8 feet. It was suspended by a cable from each corner that hooked into a large steel ring, which the cable from the crane hooked into.

I signaled to the operator, and he lifted us up to the height we needed to be and swung the cage over to the building. These were pre-finished buildings, and even though there was an inch or more of frost on it, I knew that any scratches would show up when the weather warmed up and the frost melted in the spring. He had us tight against the building and the cage was scraping along it. I signaled to the operator to swing us away from the building. We were still scraping along and suddenly, I got a terrible feeling in the pit of my stomach!

I looked up to see what the crane boom was doing and just as I looked up, I heard a noise like a shotgun blast and saw the cable break. A split second later, I heard the crash when the lift we were in hit the ground, and then I heard another crash, and my right leg started to burn like it was on fire. The load block had fallen on my leg and crushed it. This thing weighed several hundred pounds. I was trying to pull my leg out from under it, of course, to no avail. The operator tried to move the block but he couldn't budge it. He told me to just lie still and he would get someone to help.

I looked over at Mike, and he was lying flat on his back with his eyes closed. I called his name and asked him if he was ok but he didn't answer. I thought he was dead. The cage was made out of angle iron. I don't know how it happened, but somehow the top part of my body was lying outside the cage, and obviously my legs were far enough apart so that only one leg was hit.

The operator came back with some help, and they freed my leg. The medics put us on stretchers and got us inside. I asked about Mike, and they told me he was ok—just a minor injury. Good news! The medics had to cut the clothing off my leg so they could see what needed to be done. I knew it was bad because people would come over, look down at my leg, drop their head and walk away.

My leg was hurting bad, and I asked the medics to give me something for the pain but they told me they had already given me all they could. I wondered what it would have felt like if they hadn't given me anything! They put two tourniquets on my thigh; I was bleeding quite profusely it seems.

Our living quarters were Atco units, which were pre-constructed housing units, and there were two men to a room. My roommate John was also a Christian, and I asked him to pray that I wouldn't bleed to death (which at the time seemed like a real possibility). He assured me that he would.

Fortunately for us, when this accident happened there was a Great Northern Airlines twin-engine cargo plane on the ramp. The "ramp" is an area on the airport where pilots warm up their engines, check their instruments, do their preflight inspections, and prepare for flight—which in this case was back to Anchorage. They held the plane up until they could get us on board. I say fortunately, because later they told me that there are times when Camp Lonely gets socked in with fog for days at a time, but today they were able to fly.

Earlier in this writing, I mentioned that all of that hiking and packing out caribou meat would have another benefit later on. The doctors told me later that I had gone through three stages of shock, and that if I hadn't been in such good physical condition I would never have survived that accident. I believe that God intervened weather wise, and in every way so that I did survive.

They got us on the plane and we took off for Anchorage. A short time later, I saw one of the medics walk over to a crewman. He took his belt off and handed it to the medic. He came back and put another tourniquet on my thigh. They were having trouble getting the bleeding stopped. A short time later the pilot came on the intercom and said, "Hey guys, we just lost an engine, but the plane is light, and I think we can make it to Anchorage." Well! About then I was thinking I should have stayed in bed that morning!

I was lying on a gurney in the hospital corridor. The accident had happened at 11:30 a.m. and it was now around 7 p.m. A doctor came over with some papers in his hand. He explained that they were getting ready to take me into the operating room. He said they didn't know what they would find, and he needed me to sign some papers to allow them to do whatever was needed, and that they might have to take my leg.

Well, I really didn't have any choice, but I told him that I sure wanted to keep my leg! I signed the papers. As it turned out, they didn't operate that night. As I understand it, they rigged up a device to pump a saline solution through the leg below the knee, to try to clean the arteries out. The doctors checked it often, and we all hoped for the best.

We had some neighbors seven miles up the highway who had a telephone. When I filled out the papers to take the job with Alaska General, I gave them their phone number. When the accident happened, they called my neighbors, and Bud answered the phone. They asked him if he knew me, and if he knew where I lived. He told them he did, and they asked him if he could contact my wife. He told them he could.

Bud came in on his snow machine. Betty was quite surprised because we had wanted him to come out for a visit and this was the first time he had come out. She told him that I wasn't home, and that I would be very disappointed that I missed him. He asked Betty to please sit down, he had some news about me.

Bud told her that I had been in an accident. He didn't know how serious it was, but the company I was working for had called him, and asked him to get her to the airport in Delta as soon as possible, because they were sending a Lear Jet to fly her to Anchorage. He told her that they were flying me to Anchorage from Camp Lonely. She hurried and got her stuff together and went with him. Betty said that it was a fast trip. She was in my room at Providence Hospital by midnight. She said I talked to her, but I don't remember seeing her until the next day.

Two days later my toes started turning black. They began preparing me for surgery. I asked the doctor to please try to save my knee. I had known some above-knee amputees, and I knew that if I at least had my knee joint, where and how I was living would be a lot easier if I still had my knee. When I woke up back in the Intensive Care Unit, I asked Betty if they took my leg, because I could still feel it. She nodded her head yes. The doctors were able to save my knee.

Mike came to see me while I was in the hospital. That was the first time I'd seen him since the accident. I asked him why he didn't answer me when I asked him if he was o.k., and that I thought he was dead, and he just said, "Oh, I just didn't feel like talking." He was a fine young man, and I was glad that he wasn't seriously hurt.

The doctors told me that I would have to stay in Anchorage for a few more months, so that I could be there for checkups after I was released from the hospital. The company I had been working for rented an apartment for us and gave us a car to use. We certainly appreciated that very, very much.

Betty was able to come home and see how the kids were doing, and she even brought them to Anchorage where we celebrated Christmas of 1976 right there in the hospital. During the winter we went home to check on things as often as we could. The kids were doing fine. Betty was able to get a job with Alyeska Pipeline Service Company. That was a big help financially. Later, she got a job with Sohio, a branch of British Petroleum, which was one of the companies that built the Trans–Alaska oil pipeline.

All we needed now was for me to get healed up and get back to our cabin in the woods and get back to living. My first prosthetist was right there in Anchorage. He fit me with a temporary socket. My leg was still very swollen, and that would help to reduce the swelling. It would be several months yet before he could fit me with a more permanent prosthesis.

Well, I won't bore you with all the details of my recovery, the literally hundreds of hours that I spent in prosthetists' offices in Alaska, California and Seattle, Washington: the months away from home that were required, and the frustration of it all. I will tell you that it was five years before I finally got a prosthesis that I could get around on that didn't hurt too bad. Every step I took, I was aware of my problem. My stump was very short, and that made the fitting process very difficult.

I thought at one time that it would be better to lose an arm than a leg; at least I would be able to get around. After a while though, I realized that even though it was difficult getting around, that once I got to wherever it was I wanted to go I had two hands to do things with. I realized that I could still play music, cut firewood, drive my snow machine, run my trapline, and anything else that requires two hands.

I made the statement once that, "If it's just a matter of stumbling around down here for a few more years, I can handle that!" Well, by the Grace of God, I'm on my 40th year of "stumbling around" and I'm still going! Praise God!

26 Life Goes On

I want to tell you of a humorous event that happened after I was able to get out on the trapline again. We cut many miles of trails, so we only cut them as wide as we absolutely had to, to get our snow machine through. I had a Skidoo Elan snow machine at the time. It was about the smallest machine that Skidoo made. The running boards were not wide enough to get my big boots up under the cowling, so they just stuck out sideways.

One day, I came up to one of my sets and noticed that I had to make some adjustments. I got off the snow machine and almost fell on my face! On the prosthesis that I was wearing, the foot was bolted on. Somewhere along the line, my foot must have hit something, and it had turned around so the toe was pointing backward. A real surprise! I told Betty about it and we both had a good laugh. I told her that if someone was ever tracking me and I wanted to get away, I'd just turn that foot around, and they wouldn't know which way I was going.

I read a book once called "The Mad Trapper of Rat River" by Dick North. It's a story of a man the Canadian Mounties were chasing. It was wintertime, and at one point in the chase, they said that he put his snowshoes on backward and they tracked him for a long ways before they realized what he had done. He was able to avoid capture for quite a while longer by doing that. He had to have been some kind of a man. When they finally got him, they said he was carrying a 200 pound pack, as well as a rifle and some other stuff, and he avoided capture for several months, living off the land in the dead of winter.

Well, getting around in the woods in the summertime and hunting season was difficult. I decided what I needed was a horse. I bought one from a guy in Anchorage. He was going to bring him to my place, but he was having a difficult time getting the horse to load. He offered to give my money back, but I figured that once I got him home he would work out fine. I didn't know much about horses, but I had a neighbor who did, and I asked him to come over to see my horse and give me some pointers on how to handle him. He was still a little wild, but we got along ok. I didn't have a corral or shed for him yet, so I just staked him out in the woods.

One Sunday when we returned from church, I noticed that he was down. I thought he was just resting, but I went out to check. I don't know what happened. I thought he might have stepped in a hole or something; anyway he had a broken leg. I dispatched him and went over to the neighbors to see if they wanted him. They sent some guys over and butchered him and took him home.

I experimented with several ATV's and they were ok, but limited as to where they could go. In the summer of 1979 our daughter Eileen saw an ad in the paper of a guy who had a mule for sale. She got word to me and I checked it out. The mule had been wintered in Delta Junction. His owner was a hunting guide up at Wiseman, Alaska. He told me the mule was around 20 years old and he wanted to retire him. He was big, measuring 16.3 hands. The owner told me that he was gentle and I could pack him, ride him, crawl under his belly, or whatever I wanted to do with him. I found that to be true after I had him for a while.

In my opinion, mules are wonderful animals. He died in August of 1986. I had him for seven years, and I really loved that old mule! We had many experiences hunting and otherwise. With the help of Virgil and Juanita, and their two boys, I built a large corral, about 50 yards long and 30 yards wide. I also built him a 12x12 foot shed. He used it some, but most of the time he stayed outside. This was just what I needed. I forgot to tell you his name. It was Festus. He was named after one of Matt Dillon's deputies — remember the TV show "Gunsmoke?"

I really loved that old mule. I treated him well, and he treated me the same. There was only one time that he showed his temper to me. The corral was about 75 yards from the cabin. Every morning he stood by his grain box waiting for me to come out and give him his morning feeding. It was comical to hear him. When he saw me coming out of the cabin he started making his noises. It wasn't a whinny like horses make, and it wasn't a bray like donkeys make, it was sort of a mixture of both.

Festus 1979

Every morning the first thing I did was give him his grain, then put some hay out for him. This morning though, I decided to just go over to pet him, scratch his ears and talk to him a little before I gave him his grain. He did not like that at all—he wanted his grain. He swung his head around and nipped me on the shoulder. Quick as a wink, I slapped him with my open hand on the side of his neck. It startled him, and he took off and ran to the far side of the corral. I tested him later that same way, and he never tried that again.

Festus by his feeder

27 Hunting the High Lonesome

With Festus, I could ride all the way to my caribou camp for some hunting in what the old Mountain Men called the "High Lonesome." I went up hunting on the 29th of August that year (1979).

Bob's camp on the Macomb Plateau with Festus grazing

There is an old horse trail that goes west up a drainage to Horn Mountain. That is the route I took on this trip. I cut a different and much better trail up the plateau, which I will explain later. The horse trail was good going for Festus. It was, however, the long way around to where I wanted to hunt, which was Berry Creek Ridge.

When we got to the top, I wanted to cut straight across to the southeast, but Festus didn't want to go that way. I didn't know why so I urged him on. As we moved along, he suddenly stopped. His big ears pointed straight ahead. I figured there was something out there, but I couldn't see anything. Finally I looked through my binoculars and there was a lone caribou about a mile and a half away. Festus was an amazing animal.

Festus still didn't want to go the way I wanted to go, but I kept insisting. He reluctantly moved ahead. We went about 25 yards, and suddenly, he was in muck up to his knees. I took my feet out of the stirrups in case he went down, and started turning him around. Before we got out of the muck, he went down. I jumped off and led him out. He knew the ground was bad. I learned a lesson from that.

You have to get to know mules. You can make a horse do just about anything you want him to, but mules have a very strong sense of "self-preservation." You have to learn when there is danger, and when they just "don't wanna." You have to know the difference. A lot of people think they are being stubborn, but there is a difference. Also, mules have a very good memory. If you treat them right, fine, but if you don't, they'll remember, and when you're not expecting it, they'll get even!

Well, due to that muck we had to take the long way around. We got over to Berry Creek Ridge and were walking along at a leisurely pace. I looked behind us and about a hundred yards away was a young bull caribou sort of following along. I got down, got my rifle out of the scabbard, and got ready to shoot. There was nothing to tie the reins to, so I just let them hang down. I wondered if Festus would still be there after I shot. I shot the caribou and turned around to see where Festus was; he was still standing there. What a relief. I had visions of him running off when I shot.

Before I went up hunting, my neighbor Geoff told me he might see me up there because he was going up to try to get a grizzly bear. There were lots of bears on Macomb Plateau so he had a good chance of getting one. It was just about dark when I shot the caribou, so I just field dressed him and propped the cavity open with a stick so the meat would cool. I fed Festus, had some supper myself, and went to sleep. The next morning I was skinning the caribou out and Geoff walked up. He was camped below my camp, and said he was sitting outside his tent drinking a cup of tea when he saw me on the skyline moving around. We talked awhile, I gave

135

him a piece of tenderloin, and he disappeared. I went on about my job. He came back a little later and said, "Boy, that sure is good meat!" He also had moved his camp up to where I was.

High Lonesome Caribou

I decided to leave my camp up there to make it easier on Festus, and planned to go back up and get it in a couple of days. Geoff stayed to hunt. We got back to the cabin just fine, and I hung the meat up to age a little. The next day I had to go to Delta to get some supplies.

That night it snowed, and up on top of the plateau it was like a blizzard. It was unusual for the end of August. Geoff didn't have his snowshoes with him so he hightailed it back to his cabin. He had to leave fast so he left his camp there. Festus and I went up the next day to get my camp. I couldn't believe the snow…and it was still coming down. In places Festus was belly deep in it, but we had no trouble getting to camp. It was late afternoon and I had planned to spend the night anyway and come out the next day, so all was well.

I woke up about 6 a.m. and the wind was really howling, blowing the snow horizontally. I gave Festus some grain, fried up some caribou steaks that I had brought with me, had some coffee and looked out again. The visibility was about 50 yards. There was a ridge on the far side of the valley about a mile away, and I told myself that if it cleared up enough so that I could see that ridge, I'd pack up and head for home. I went back to sleep for a while.

About two o'clock in the afternoon I looked out and I could see that ridge so I started packing up. Festus amazed me! All I could see of the trail we had made the day before were very slight dimples in the snow. Some stretches I couldn't see any signs of it at all, but Festus went back out the exact same way that he had come in. He even went around the same side of rocks that he did coming up.

I also packed up Geoff's camp and took it to him. It was after dark when we got to his cabin. His dog started barking and Geoff came out. I said, "Hey Geoff, Festus and I went up and got my camp, and I brought yours out too. I hope you don't mind!" Well, I knew he didn't mind—I was just having some fun. He was one happy guy! He said he was planning to go up and get it when it stopped snowing, but he was really glad that now he didn't have to. We got his stuff down, and went in and had some coffee. There is nothing in this old world better than good friends! He said that he hadn't seen any bears.

In those early years, several families had CB (citizen band) radios. We had two call times a day, 12 noon and 8 p.m. We all checked in at those times to keep up with what was happening in our lives. One night Geoff told us that he had shot a big bull moose up in the valley above our cabin. He said that he had field dressed it and propped it open to cool, but it was getting dark so he had to leave it at that.

Geoff, Judy and Betty with Geoff's moose

It was unfamiliar territory to him, and he didn't want to get caught in the dark, and have to stumble around trying to find his way back to his cabin. He said the way he came down was difficult, and he certainly wouldn't be able to pack the moose out that way. He asked me if I knew of a trail up there from my side.

I told him that there was a long hogs back ridge that rose more gradually than the rest of the terrain, but I didn't think there was an actual trail. It started about a half mile south of our cabin. I told him I would have to cut a trail in order to get Festus up there to pack his moose out. We decided that the next morning, he and his wife Jody, Billy and Judy, and Betty would go up and start working on the moose, and I would take Festus and start cutting the trail.

There were no big trees so the cutting was quite easy. I had to cut it at least six feet wide. Festus was a big guy, and when the panniers were full of meat it took that much room to get him through. I got about halfway up that day. They each packed some meat down to meet us, and we came back to the cabin. We went back the next day and Festus and I got to the top.

We got the rest of the meat loaded. I was standing in front of Festus holding him, and Geoff came up with the antlers, a big 50" rack. When Festus saw that, he decided that he didn't want that big thing on him and he bolted. He knocked me down. I was still holding the reins, but I was flat on my back between his front legs hollering, "Whoa, Festus, Whoa!" He stopped and stood still. Good boy! Geoff tied the antlers to the pack and we headed for home.

From then on, I used that trail all the time. It was solid ground and an easy climb for my old mule. You might be wondering if the meat would keep up there for two days. Yes, absolutely! This was the middle of September, and the weather was plenty cool enough to keep it. The only danger was bears, or some other varmint that would get into the meat. That's the chance you have to take sometimes. Usually when we got a moose we were able to get it out the same day, no problem, but this was an extraordinary situation. We did get all of the meat out, and nothing was wasted.

28 "I Don't Wanna!"

I had a lot of experiences with Festus and I'd like to tell you of some more. I had a trail that went downstream on the East Fork. We were walking along one day when a grouse flew up right close to him. He never missed a step; just kept walking along as though it never happened. His former owner was a hunting guide, so Festus had probably experienced that type of thing before.

One time we were walking along the same trail, coming home. Betty was working in the garden raking up leaves. She had a black plastic bag full of leaves sitting close to the trail. As soon as we got to where Festus could see it, he stopped, his big ears pointing forward. To him, I guess it looked like a black bear. I told him it was ok, that it was just a bag of leaves. He just stood there. I called to Betty and asked her to move the bag. She did and ole Festus started walking toward the corral.

When we built the corral, we had three spruce poles about 10 feet long for the gate. All one had to do is slide the poles over to get in or out. I'm sure Festus had seen that setup before, and had watched as I went in and out. One pole was about a foot off the ground, the top pole about five feet high and another pole between them.

One day while I was away, Betty was working in the garden and she heard, "clomp, clomp!" She looked up and here came Festus down the trail. He had slid the top and center poles over, stepped over the bottom one, and had come to see Betty. At first she was afraid—how was she going to get him back in the corral?

She thought quickly. She went out to the hay barn and put some grain in a can and started shaking the can. He couldn't get back there fast enough. She got him back in the corral just like that. She tied the poles in place with binder twine so he couldn't do that again. I don't believe that he would have gone anywhere anyway. We took good care of him, but we had to keep him under control.

One bad habit Festus had, was to stop and eat when he saw something delicious (at least to a mule). I didn't mind him snatching leaves off the branches as we went by, but I didn't want him to stop and eat. One time when he stopped, I reached over and broke a branch off the tree about three feet long, stripped the leaves off of it, and switched his belly. He took off like I had really hurt him. As long as I held the switch, he wouldn't stop; he'd just strip the leaves off and keep walking.

I tried many times to throw that switch away without him knowing it, but nothing worked. I tried holding my arm straight down and letting the switch just slip out of my hand and I tried dropping it with my other hand. But he was a sharp old guy and always knew when I dropped it, because when he came to the next bunch of leaves, he would stop and eat. I'd break off another switch and he would start walking again.

I saw a video about mules once, and it showed how a mule's eyes are set on each side of his head so that he can see all four feet, and know right where to place each foot. I believe that's probably why Festus could see every time I dropped the switch. The first year I had Festus, I had him shod. The shoes caused him to slip on the rocks and made it difficult for him. After that first hunting season was over I had the shoes removed and never had him shod again.

One time some folks from Delta came to Macomb Plateau to hunt caribou. They had horses, and one night one of them broke his rope or pulled the stake and came down off the plateau. They came down and looked for him but could find no trace of him. Festus and I made several trips over there to look for it. I thought the horse might come to Festus, and I could get a rope on him and hold him for his owner. We never saw any sign of him though, even after the snow came.

I think it was about the last trip that we went over. Anyway, the creek was freezing up so it was probably October. My trail followed the East Fork for a half mile, then crossed it, and on through the woods to the farm, then on to the trail that went up to Horn Mountain where the horse disappeared from.

Well, we got to the creek and found it frozen over. I decided I should check to make sure the ice was safe for Festus to cross. There was 3 inches of solid ice, but about an inch above that was a thin layer of shelf ice, and when I stepped on it, it made a "tinkle, tinkle" sound.

No problem, there was solid ice beneath it. I got back in the saddle, and urged Festus on. He got right up to the creek bank and stiffened his front legs. He would turn left, and he would turn right, but he was not going to cross that creek. He was not being stubborn. He heard that "tinkle, tinkle" sound when I stepped on the ice, and thought he might break through and get hurt if he stepped on it.

I walked him back about 20 feet, and sat there a couple minutes to let him calm down, and tried it again. Same thing. I tried a couple more times to no avail. So we came back to the cabin, took our trail to the north and turned west. Where the pipeline right-of-way crossed the creek it was dry, so no problem. We went over and wandered around through the woods for a while. We didn't see any sign of the horse. There was snow on the ground so if he was around we could have tracked him.

It was starting to get dark so I decided we needed to get on our way home. It was a lot shorter going to the farm and hitting my trail there. I figured that since we were headed for home and some grain, that Festus would cross the creek. We got to the creek—same thing! He was not about to cross that creek! I had to go back to the farm, out to the pipeline, east to our trail, and home. We didn't go over looking for the horse anymore. By that time, I thought the wolves had gotten him, he had starved, or frozen to death. No one ever did find him. However, my story doesn't end there.

The next summer I decided to go for a ride. I saddled Festus up and headed down the creek trail. The snow was all gone. There was absolutely no ice on the creek. I turned him toward the creek, and when he got up to it, he stiffened his front legs, turned left, turned right, but he wasn't going to cross that creek!

I walked him back a ways, sat there for a minute or so, and I told him it was ok, so let's go. He got right up to the creek again and stopped. He was not going to cross that creek! I walked him back a ways, got off, and walked up in front of him. I was holding the reins short, and I got my face right up to about a foot from his big head, looked him right in his big brown eye, and said in a stern voice, "Festus, this is summertime, there is no snow, and there is no ice on that creek. You got away with this last fall, but you are not getting away with it now!"

All the time I was staring him right in the eye. "And Festus, you ARE going to cross that creek! Do you understand me?" I looked him in the eye for a few more seconds, got back in the saddle, nudged him in the ribs and said, "Let's go!" He walked up to the creek and right on across; he never even hesitated.

As I mentioned before, I had to learn when he was trying to avoid hurting himself, and when he just "didn't wanna." How could I not love that old guy? I still think about him, and it's been 28 years since he died. I miss him, especially when hunting season comes around.

One hunting season a friend wanted to go up caribou hunting. I already had mine, but I suggested a spot for him to go and told him that Festus and I would come up the next day, and if he had a caribou we would pack it out for him. I had to go back up anyway to get my camp. Whenever I got a caribou, I usually left my camp there to make it easier on my "old timer," as I referred to him sometimes. I would go back up and get it later.

My friend had decided to not go where I suggested; and he just stayed around my camp. When Festus and I got there, he decided to walk around a little. Since I already had my meat, I put my rifle in the tent, got my spotting scope out, and set it up. It was a beautiful sunny day and I was enjoying just sitting out in front of the tent drinking a cup of coffee.

From where my camp was, to the west about a mile or so was where the main branch of Dry Creek starts. To the east and just a little closer was the head of the East Fork. Coming up from the head of Dry Creek I saw a dark animal running toward the East Fork gorge. I thought it was a black bear but when I looked at it through my scope it was a large, silver tip grizzly! He was just loping along and his long hair was sort of flowing back and forth as he ran; a beautiful animal.

I could take him if he got close enough so I went into the tent to get my rifle. I didn't think he would drop down into the East Fork, but that he would turn when he got there and come up towards me. Ha! Wrong! When I came back out of the tent, he was gone. I never saw him again. I was a little disappointed, but that's the way hunting is. My friend didn't get a caribou, so I packed up my camp and we came back out. I did get a nice grizzly later though.

One year, Billy shot a black bear and decided to have a bear barbeque. Of course, we were all invited and I decided to put my Mountain Man costume on and ride Festus in. We had a friend from Anchorage whose daughter lived on Dry Creek. He was a long time buck-skinner and had shot muzzle-loaders for a lot of years. He was at the barbeque, and when I came out of the woods riding Festus, with my long rifle and all my gear, he said I looked like some old Mountain Man riding in from the long ago. We had a good laugh. The barbeque was a success and everyone had a good time

29 Our First Grizzly

Just southeast of Dot Lake there was an old trail that went back toward Monte Lake. I had a track machine called a Kidd. I think it was made for use in the rice paddies of Vietnam.

We had two days of moose season left, and Betty and I decided to go out and try to get one. We drove down to that trail, unloaded the machine, and started down through the woods. We could see the trail when we started but soon lost it. It was an old trail and the brush was grown up, so it was difficult to see. We ended up on a ridge back in there four or five miles, and could go no further. No problem. We set up camp. We still had lots of daylight so we decided to hunt for a while.

Betty went west and I went east. This was the 13th of September. I walked along the ridge for a couple hundred yards or so, and sat down where I had a good view of the side of the ridge. At the bottom of the ridge, the ground leveled off into a grassy area with clumps of alders and willows. There were four or five inches of dead leaves on the ground, and it was comfortable. The warm sun was shining down on me and making me sleepy. I had been sick with the flu for several days and was pretty tired. I laid my rifle down close by and leaned back against a tree and closed my eyes.

I'm not sure if I went to sleep, but suddenly I sat upright, eyes wide open. I must have heard a noise. About a hundred yards below me I saw what I thought was a moose. It wasn't! It was a grizzly! He was standing up on his hind feet with his front feet up on a windfall. I reached for my rifle. He either saw me move, or heard the leaves rustle when I picked my rifle up. He made a loud "woof" and took off.

He got to a small open place just before he went into the thick trees. He stopped, stood up on his hind legs, and looked up at me. I put the crosshairs of my scope on the center of his chest and fired. He dropped down on all fours and disappeared into the brush. He

146

was going in the direction of our camp. I was very sure that I had hit him, and I thought that when Betty heard my shot, she would be coming over to where I was. I didn't want her running into a wounded bear, so I hightailed it for camp to head her off. I had read about and heard stories of hunters tracking wounded bears into the brush, so I decided to play it safe.

I met Betty at camp and told her I'd shot a grizzly, and I was sure I'd hit him, but that we would have a cup of coffee before we went looking for him. I knew that if the bullet went in where the crosshairs on my scope were, he would only live a few minutes but I wanted to give him a little time anyway. I guess it was about an hour when we went back to where I shot him and looked for his trail.

I could not believe what little evidence there was that a wounded grizzly had gone through there. We could track him through the scuffed up leaves for a little ways, and then there was nothing. We couldn't even find any blood. Back in Michigan while hunting deer, if we had a wounded buck in a swamp and we couldn't find him, we'd start circling. A small circle then a little larger one, and it usually worked — we would usually find him.

I decided to try that on this bear. About the third time around I spotted a leaf with one red spot on it. Blood! We moved slowly and soon found more. We came to a really thick place, and I had Betty stand ready while I went in. I went in ten yards or so and had her come in. I went on a little farther and there he was. It's always wise to be very careful in a situation like this — you want to be sure he's dead before you walk up to him! I picked up a long stick and walked up slowly and carefully behind him. I put the stick in his eye and there was no reaction, so I knew he was dead.

Betty came up and I was going to have her take my picture with the bear. I tried to pick his head up, but rigor mortis had already set in, and he was as stiff as a board. He died within minutes after he was shot. He must have been standing a little sideways to me because the bullet went in right in the center of his rib cage and came out about four inches to the left of his backbone. It went through his left lung though, and that's what did him in.

By this time, it was getting dark. I was trying to skin the bear with Betty holding a flashlight for me. Well, I'm sure you can guess how that was working out. Also, I got to thinking that there might be other bears around, and the smell of blood and fresh meat just might bring them in. Not a comfortable thought! I built two fires about eight feet on each side of the bear to keep critters away, and it also gave me light for skinning.

It had started to rain lightly, and it was getting miserable. It was three o'clock in the morning by the time we finished the job. I was able to get the track machine right down to the bear, so we didn't have to pack him out on our backs. We brought all the meat out. We ate some and gave Virgil, Billy and Ed some of it. We all enjoyed the meat; it was very good! This bear must have been feeding on roots and berries. Not all grizzly meat is fit to eat. If they have been eating rotten meat, they don't taste good.

In Alaska, we are not required to salvage the meat of a grizzly bear for that reason. It is required to salvage the head and the hide. We have to take them to a Fish and Game office to have them sealed. They put a metal tag on an ear and on the skull with the year of the kill, and put the information in their records. They also take a small tooth from the lower jaw. They can determine the age and physical condition of the bear from that tooth.

After they are sealed, you are allowed to have them. I boiled the meat off the skull and I still have it sitting up on a shelf in my garage. I fleshed and salted the hide, rolled it up and tied it. I wanted to have a rug made from it but didn't have the finances at that time. I put it away and forgot about it. Years later I got it out and found that bugs had gotten into it and it was ruined. I felt bad about that; it was a nice hide.

30 Adventures with Family and Friends

A humorous event happened one time when our granddaughter Amy was visiting us. I was going to take the snow machine and visit a neighbor. When I mentioned it, Pam and Amy wanted to go with me. I hitched the sled up to the machine. Pam got in the box and Amy wanted to ride on the back of the sled. I told her to hang on tight. She said ok. She was 7 or 8 years old at the time.

We stayed longer than I had planned, and it was dark by the time we started back. Every few minutes I'd look back to see if the girls were still with me. One time I looked back and didn't see Amy. I asked Pam where she was, and Pam said she was there just a minute ago! I shut the machine off and was going to back down the trail to find her when I heard, "Graaaandpaaaa!" in a tiny little voice. I hollered back and went to meet her. She was scared, and had seen some big tracks in the snow.

The snow was a couple feet deep. When the rabbits ran around you could only see big holes in the snow. They could have been moose tracks too. Also, when I shut the snow machine off the light went out and it was really dark and, to a little girl, very scary! She thought they were some kind of monster tracks. She was not hurt and was happy she found us.

I thought that she had fallen off the sled, but sometime later we were talking about it, and she told me what really happened. She said that the snow machine started slowing down, and she thought we were going to get stuck, so she jumped off to push. Just about then, the machine lurched ahead and she lost her grip and fell down in the snow.

Another time when Amy was visiting, she was playing out by the creek and suddenly started screaming. Ed ran out and saw that she had stepped on a yellow jackets nest. They were all over her. He brushed them off quickly but they both got quite a few stings.

Bob with his granddaughter Amy, 1976

When Eileen was close to giving birth to their son T.J., Amy was here for about a month. It seems that T.J. wasn't in any hurry, and the birth was taking longer than expected. We went to Delta one day and called Eileen and Amy talked to her and asked her mom how long before she could come home. She really missed them and I guess she thought she would never get back home. While she was here, Betty had Amy help her mix potting soil. Later, Eileen asked her what she had been doing and she said that she was helping grandma "make dirt." She was a lot of fun and we always enjoyed having her visit.

Ed and Eileen came down quite often. Sometimes Ed and I went fishing in a small lake nearby. We could get some nice rainbow trout there. One day we were sitting out on the lake in our boat and a red Super Cub flew over. He circled around to head into the wind, landed, and taxied over to us. The pilot climbed out, stood on one of the floats and asked to see our fishing licenses. He was the game warden! That was a real surprise. We had never seen anything like that before. Another time we were on the same lake and a cow moose came out of the brush with two newborn calves. Those little guys sure are cute.

On another trip it was early spring and the ice was just beginning to melt. There was an open lead that went halfway across the lake, and was about fifteen feet wide at the shore. I had an aluminum boat I left there for anyone who wanted to use it. We wanted to fish so we got in the boat and rowed out into the lake. The ripple from the boat was causing the ice to break up. The ice was made up of long, hollow, tube-like icicles, and when they bumped against each other it sounded just like music. Neither of us had ever seen anything like that. Alaska is full of surprises!

I was happy to leave my boat there for people to use, but one time I went over there and discovered that someone had shot a hole through it. The next winter I went over with my snow machine and dragged it out of there. As someone once remarked, "It takes all kinds!" It does, and we certainly have "all kinds!" Some folks just don't appreciate things.

Our friend Bud and his wife Billie June fished several of these small lakes often. Bud fixed a plank to scale and cut up fish on, and at one lake he even made a nice picnic table for everyone to use. They went over there later and discovered someone had cut it up for firewood.

Bud was a hunter and a trapper. Billie June also enjoyed outdoor activities, and one of her great desires was to shoot a grizzly bear. One day, one of their friends spotted a big grizzly over by the Johnson River, which was only about seven miles from their home and he went and got Billie June, and she shot it—one of the highlights of her life. She was a little gal, and the grizzly was huge, but her 30.06 rifle made them equal.

Billie June and her grizzly

Ed came down one time and we went caribou hunting. I already had mine that season, but Festus and I went up with him so if he got one we would pack it out for him. I was riding Festus and Ed was walking behind. He learned all about muskeg that day. Of course, Festus had no problem with his long legs, but it was really tough going for Ed. We made it to camp though, and he was pretty tired.

The next day he decided to go for a walk to see if there were any caribou around. He said he hadn't seen anything yet, but he was walking along the ridge above our camp and stopped to rest, and take a look around. He turned and looked behind him, and there was a young bull following him. Caribou are curious creatures, and they do things like that. Well, Ed shot him; we processed him, packed up our camp and came back to the cabin.

I've never hunted antelope, but a friend who has told me that they are very curious. Sometimes the hunter would hide himself and wave a handkerchief or other piece of cloth, and the antelope would come over to see what it was and get close enough so he could shoot it. Caribou must be from the same family, because they are that way too. I've been up there skinning out a caribou and every once in a while stand up to stretch my back, and there would be one or sometimes four or five caribou standing there 75 yards away watching me.

31 Two Horses and a Donkey

I bought two horses and a little white donkey from a former hunting guide. One of my upper Dry Creek neighbors, Dick came over, and we were going to go up on Macomb Plateau and try to get some caribou meat. I had the gelding tied to a post in the hay barn, and was trying to get a bridle on him. He was being very difficult. I kept trying and suddenly he reared up and broke the rope I had him tied with. It was a brand new ¾ inch rope. Man, that's power!

We had planned for Dick to ride him on the hunt, but when he saw that, he wasn't really sure that he wanted to do this. Well, maybe the gelding would let me get a packsaddle and a halter on him, and Dick could ride the mare. I got a rope halter on him and tied him to a post on the corral fence. We got the packsaddle on him, hung the panniers on it, and proceeded to load him. I was very careful to get each side loaded equally so the saddle wouldn't slide over to one side or the other.

We had everything loaded, and Dick walked around behind him with his sleeping bag. It spooked the horse, and he started bucking. He kept it up until everything was scattered all over the ground. I'll just say that it was a very good thing for that horse that I hadn't brought my rifle out yet. I put him back in the corral and brought the mare out. We had no trouble getting her saddled up, and we were soon on our way. It was getting late, and I wanted to get to my caribou camp before dark.

I was in the lead, and I looked back now and then to see how Dick was doing. I was trying to hurry, but I didn't want to get too far ahead. I stopped again, and didn't see him, so I turned ole Festus around and went back to see what was going on. Dick saw me coming and hollered, "she won't go!" I went back to see what could be done. We couldn't see anything wrong with her, but she wouldn't budge. Well, anyone who knows me will tell you that I'm not a patient man. I have really tried, but somehow I just haven't gotten there, at least, not yet. Maybe someday…I guess time will tell.

As I have mentioned before, Festus was a big powerful mule. I put a rope around the mare's neck, got back in the saddle, took a couple turns of the rope around the saddle horn, and gave Festus the signal to move on. When Festus goes, anything tied to him is going to go also, no question. Dick told me later that the rope tightened up and the mare's neck started stretching. It kept stretching until he thought sure that her head was going to pop right off! She started to move before that happened though!

I could see that we weren't going to make it to my camp before dark, so we just camped right there, and went on the next morning. The mare was not any better the next day and Dick had to walk. She would move with him leading her, but would not budge with him in the saddle.

The person I had bought them from told me if they didn't work out I could bring them back and get my money back, so that's what I did. I kept the donkey though because I thought I could use him for packing. I even named him "Packer!" However, as it turned out he was a useless varmint also! I'll tell you more about that later. I always said that if a man had two good mules, he could go anywhere in this country that he wanted to go, one for riding, and one for packing. Of course they should be young animals, not old ones like Festus. However, Festus worked out just fine for me.

32 The Lost Knife

In the early '80's my friend Doug, whom I had met on the Alaska Hwy in 1973, came up for a visit. Just before he left to go back home, he asked me if I needed a good hunting knife. He said that his dad made knives, and if I wanted him to make one for me to give him an idea what I wanted, and his dad would make it. I told him I would like one with an 8" drop point blade and a deer horn crown handle.

I think it was the following year; Doug came back to Alaska and gave me the knife. It was a beautiful piece of work. The blade was 8" long, 1¼" wide, about 3/16" thick at the back and tapered down to the cutting edge. The blade and tang were one piece. He used a mule deer antler crown (that's the end of the antler that is next to the skull) and it was 5 inches long, about 1¼ inch in diameter, and fastened with copper rivets. I made a sheath for it and took that knife with me on every hunt after that. I had it on my trips up on the plateau moose hunting.

One time we went moose hunting on the plateau east of our creek. My back trapline went halfway up the side of the plateau, and ended in the alders and smaller brush. We went up that trail, and then just found our way through wherever we could. I found a good place along the ridge, staked Festus out, and found a spot to sit and watch. A couple hours later I heard a cow moose coming toward me. I couldn't see her yet, but I could hear her for a long ways. She was looking for a bull and was continually bawling while she was moving along.

I got pretty excited because there was a very good chance that there was a bull following her. It was another 15 or 20 minutes before she came in sight. She passed by about 75 yards away, and I waited for a while, but no bulls showed up. I stayed a while longer and we came back. That seemed like a good place to hunt, so I went back several times. There was a stretch of the trail along the ridge where the alders were higher than I was when I was sitting in the saddle. They were quite thick and difficult to get through.

After I got back from one of my trips up there, I discovered that my knife was missing. Man, I was heartsick. I felt so bad. Well, the only thing I could do was go back up and try to find it. It would definitely be like looking for a needle in a haystack. I even prayed that I would be able to find it. We made several trips back up there just to look for that knife. We didn't find it. I didn't think there was much use to go back, but a couple days later I told Betty that I guessed I'd better try again.

We went back up there ~ole Festus and me~ I tried to go through in some kind of pattern, like a 6 or 8 foot spacing so we could cover the area better. We went slowly and I scanned the ground for some sign of the knife. There was also high grass in places, which made it difficult. We kept that up for a couple of hours. I was feeling very discouraged. We were going through an exceptionally thick place—suddenly Festus just stopped. His ears were not pointing forward like he had seen or heard something ahead. He just stood there. I was sure he had a reason to stop, but why?

I sat there in the saddle trying to figure it out. I looked all around him on the ground. About 4 feet to the left in the grass was my knife. It was sticking point first in the ground, and the handle was a little higher than the grass. It was a very emotional moment for me, and here I am thirty years later, and having a little trouble seeing this page! I got down, dropped down on my knee, and thanked God for helping us to find it. I hugged Festus' neck and thanked him—I almost could have kissed him! For a moment it seemed like he was almost human—like he was saying, "Well, you gonna get down and get your knife, or what?" He somehow must have known that I was looking for my knife. Well, I don't want to put too much into it, but to me it was a miracle that we found it.

Unfortunately, I would lose my knife again—but under much different circumstances. It was August 31, 1986. The next day was the first day of moose season, so I had all of my hunting equipment lying out and planned to get an early start the next morning. I went away for a couple hours but when I got back, I found that someone had come in my cabin and stolen all my hunting stuff. They had also gone all through the cabin and found all of my other guns and everything else of value. That knife was gone too. I had no idea who had done it; I was only gone for two hours. Had they been in the woods watching and waiting for me to leave? I don't know.

A few days later I got a call from the Alaska State Troopers, who said they had some of my guns and wanted me to come in and identify them. Seems that some folks from Fort Greely were coming home from Fairbanks, and stopped at a roadside turnout to walk their dog. The lady looked down in the brush and saw some guns and other stuff laying there in the weeds. They picked up everything they could find and took them to the State Troopers' office in Delta.

I guess the thieves were afraid they might get caught and threw a lot of the stuff out there. They had also gotten into two other cabins and stole guns, ammunition, and whatever else they could find. I got some of my stuff back, but not all of it. I never got back a .38 caliber pistol, that knife, a pair of 10 power binoculars, all my camping gear, and a lot of ammunition.

The troopers detained two suspects, but they denied knowing anything about it. I understand there is no statute of limitations on firearms robberies, so if that pistol ever shows up and the robber identified, the case can still be prosecuted. Well, that was 28 years ago so it doesn't look too promising that I will ever get it back. I hope that someday the thieves will repent, and make it right with me.

33 Quicksand!

Another time, Ed and my friend Scott from North Pole came down to hunt moose. I had spotted a nice bull up the Johnson River a few miles, and we decided to try to get him. Ed and Scott were going up in the morning, and I was going to go up a little later in the day with Festus and Packer.

Scott and Ed with Packer and Bob on Festus by the Haybarn, 1985

This was my first time to use that little donkey, and after the experience with the two horses I wasn't sure how it was going to work out. I only had the packsaddle and a halter on him. When we got to the Johnson River Bridge, he didn't want to cross it. I took a couple turns of the lead rope around my saddle horn and urged Festus on. That donkey stiffened his legs and actually slid all the way across that bridge – probably a hundred and fifty yards!

Well, we got on up the trail to Lisa Lake. The lake is about three quarters of a mile from the highway, and that's where the trail ends. From there we just had to pick our way through. It was an exasperating trip to say the least. Festus and I went on one side of a tree, and Packer went on the other. I'd have to get off, go back and bring him around, get back in the saddle, go a little farther and go through the whole process again. It was so bad that it got dark, and I spent the night in the woods.

I got to where Ed and Scott were hunting about noon the next day. They had seen a young bull, but he was in a small pond so they couldn't shoot him. We talked a while, and I asked him which way it was to camp. He pointed, and I headed to it. We went just a short distance, and suddenly Festus was in mud up to his knees. Quicksand!

I unhooked Packer's lead rope and jumped off Festus. I got to solid gravel and got Packer away. Festus rolled over on his side. He was already in the quicksand up to his belly, and I think it was instinct that made him do that. Ed came over and cut a small spruce tree, laid it on the quicksand, crawled out and got the saddle off Festus. We got a rope around Festus' neck and when he would get back on his feet and try to get out; we pulled on the rope thinking that we could help him.

It didn't help, though, because he would rear up trying to get his front legs out of the quicksand, and by pulling on the rope we were just working against him. Festus would lie there on his side and rest, and about every 10 minutes or so he would roll over on his feet and struggle to get out — to no avail.

I was talking to the Lord again, and asked Him to help my old friend. He had been in that quicksand for about an hour. That water was cold, probably not more than 40° or so, and I thought his body temperature must be getting low. From what I've already told you about Festus, you might be able to feel some of the heartache that I was feeling. My thoughts were that if he stayed in there much longer, probably the best thing to do would be to put him out of his misery and leave him. I stood there watching and praying.

Suddenly, Festus rolled up on his feet and climbed right up out of there! I was sure surprised! What a joy. What an answer to my prayers! I took him over to camp, wiped him down, and dried him off as well as I could. I didn't have a blanket for him, but I had some sheet plastic. I wrapped him with that and tied some ropes around him to hold it on. It would at least keep the wind off him, and might help to get him warmed up. Well, the old timer (as I sometimes called him) survived that and we had some more adventures. We didn't get a moose, but we all survived to hunt again.

The thing that amazed me about this experience was how the area where the quicksand was looked just like the rest of the riverbed. It was all gravel and there was nothing to indicate that there was quicksand. It was an area about fifteen feet in diameter. Even Festus did not recognize the danger.

I had another experience with quicksand. Karl had a riverboat and we used to run up and down the Johnson Slough hunting moose. Over the course of several years we got two nice bulls. We decided one year to take the boat on the Tanana River, maybe we could find a moose. There was a good place to launch the boat at the confluence of the Johnson and Tanana rivers.

We headed upstream, looking for moose sign along the way. We spotted some pretty fresh looking tracks in the sand on a small island. Karl steered the boat over to the bank and we got out. He tied the boat to a tree and we started following the tracks. We had to walk along a sloping bank for a ways, and then we got to a place where it flattened out. Karl remarked, "This is a lot better, nice and solid." I was walking a few yards behind him.

When I got to the flat place, I stepped down right where he had stepped and immediately sank in the mud up to my ankles. I couldn't believe what was happening. I put my other foot down to try to lift the other one out and it sank deeper. I didn't say anything to Karl because I had no idea that I couldn't get out of there.

Karl had gotten about 50 yards ahead of me. He looked back and saw me struggling and came back to help me. By that time I was up to my knees in the quicksand. The more I struggled, the deeper I went. There was nothing that I could get a hold of to try to pull myself out. No tree branches, no vines, nothing. Karl came over and grabbed my hands to help me, and when he tried to pull me out, he started sinking too. He had to let go and get out of there quick.

By that time I was in well over my knees. I was able to stay calm, under the circumstances, but I told Karl I didn't think I was going to get out of there. I really didn't! My situation sure looked pretty hopeless. If we didn't think of something quick I was going to disappear!

We had some rope in the boat, but that was 20 minutes away and Karl didn't want to leave me for fear that when he got back I would be gone. He found some half rotten tree limbs that were laying around and started breaking them up and throwing them to me. I pushed them down in the quicksand. The pieces were three to four inches in diameter and a foot and a half long. I put ten or twelve pieces in the quicksand before they stopped sinking. I was then able to get my left knee up on top of them.

Quicksand is strange stuff. It's so easy to sink in, but after you're in it, it packs around your legs so tight that it's almost like concrete. I balanced myself on my left knee and tried to pull my right leg up. I couldn't budge it. The prosthesis that I was wearing had two steel bars molded into the fiberglass leg. The bars were hinged at the knee and came up another foot with heavy leather that laced up to hold it tight to my thigh.

Since I didn't have an ankle that would bend, I was trying to pull the leg out straight up, but the toe was holding it down. The prosthesis also had a belt fastened to it to help hold it on. I unfastened the belt, pulled my leg out of the prosthesis, and I was able to crawl out of the quicksand with Karl helping me.

He had a long stick, which I grabbed with one hand and I paddled with the other until I could crawl over to solid ground. Karl was able to get my prosthesis out of the quicksand and he washed it off in the river for me. Again the Lord heard me and helped me.

There was absolutely no indication of quicksand here either. Karl stepped on it before I did, and it felt solid to him. I was thinking about this later, wondering what a person could do in this situation if he was alone when it happened. I think that if a guy was going to hunt alone in these types of places, it would be a good thing to have 25 or 30 feet of ¼ inch nylon rope with him. He could tie the rope around his rifle, through the trigger guard, and throw it up into the brush. The rifle might get tangled up in the brush, and he could pull himself out of there. Something to think about!

The rivers in Alaska are very dangerous during both the summer and the winter. There are places in the rivers where whirlpools keep the ice thin around them. The rivers get a lot of snow machine traffic, especially the folks traveling from village to village. They travel many miles on the rivers, and every winter people die from breaking through the ice.

Another thing that makes the creeks and rivers dangerous is that after they freeze up, the water level drops. There can be a space of just a few inches to more than eight feet from the bottom of the ice to the water.

One example of that is an experience I had when I was coming down my trapline right here on the East Fork. My trapline runs right on the creek because the banks are too steep and brushy, and it's impossible to use them. I was riding along and suddenly the ice broke beneath me.

It was three feet down to the water, and about a foot and a half of water. Fortunately, I wasn't pulling my sled that day. The back of the snow machine dropped down, but the skis stayed up on the ice. I got my feet wet, but was otherwise unhurt.

I always carried a rope block and tackle with me as well as a couple of light chains. I found an alder about 3 inches in diameter, hooked a chain around it and hooked the other block to the snow machine bumper. I tightened the rope as tight as I could get it. I cut a small tree, about an inch in diameter that had a small branch on one end. I hooked the rear of the snow machine and lifted it. The machine scooted ahead two or three inches. I tightened the rope again as tight as I could get it, and lifted on the back of the snow machine again. It scooted ahead another two or three inches. I repeated that process until it was back on top of the ice. It worked well.

This was not a life-threatening situation compared to the rivers. When someone breaks through river ice they rarely get out alive. The current carries them downstream under the ice, and they can't get out. Alaska is a wonderful, beautiful, great land, but it is also a dangerous land. As it is with any wild place, one has to learn its ways, and always be aware of his surroundings.

34 Stranded!

Karl and I had quite an experience while moose hunting on the Johnson Slough. This slough is a river channel that comes off the Tanana River and runs six or seven miles and then runs back into the Tanana. Karl, his son Flori, and I were hunting on the slough. We were going slow and scanning the riverbanks ahead for signs of moose. I would be the shooter because Karl was operating the boat. Flori was along for the experience and to help if we were fortunate enough to get a moose.

The hunting regulations say that when hunting from a boat, the motor has to be shut off and all forward motion of the boat from the effects of the motor must stop before it's legal to shoot. Flori was sitting on the seat ahead of me and to my right. I cautioned him that if I got a chance to shoot, he should sit still and cover his ears. He said he would.

Bob scans the riverbanks for moose, 1993*

I guess we'd been on the river for an hour or so when we rounded a bend, and saw a nice bull moose about a hundred and fifty yards on the left side that had come down to the river for a drink. Karl shut the motor off and I got ready to shoot. The boat was still rocking a little, but all forward motion had stopped. I shot and missed him. There was a six-foot bank behind him, and I saw and heard the bullet hit the mud. The bull turned and started up the bank. I shot again. He kept on going up the bank and disappeared.

I was very sure I had hit him. The crosshairs of my scope were right behind his left shoulder when my rifle fired. Karl started the motor and got us up there as quickly as he could. I jumped out of the boat and scrambled up the bank. The bull was nowhere in sight. I figured that if he was wounded that he would head for the thickest cover he could find. I took off back into the brush. Karl tied the boat and he and Flori began searching. I hadn't seen any sign at all. A few minutes later I heard them holler that they had found him. Instead of going back 90 degrees from the river, he had gone off about 45 degrees to the southeast.

He had only gone about 75 yards and dropped. That's the only problem with lung shots: they can go a ways after being shot. But a lung shot doesn't ruin any meat, so that's why I like to use it whenever I can. Also, if you get a hole in their lungs, you won't lose them since they can't go very far. We were very happy hunters. Karl said that he was going back to the boat to get his camera. I said ok and told him I'd start working on the moose.

He came back a few minutes later. He had a strange look on his face, and I asked him if something was wrong. He said, "The boat's gone!" It seems that in his hurry to look for the moose, he had tied the boat off to a small sapling that was growing out of the riverbank. With the current of the river pushing against the boat, the sapling was pulled out of the mud and our boat left without us! Karl's very expensive camera was lying on his seat. My binoculars, some extra ammo, and some other gear were lying on my seat. The ground we were on was actually a large island with the slough on the south side and the Tanana River on the north. We were stranded. It was going to be a long night.

I had asked Betty to meet us where we would come off the river at 9:00 pm, and she waited there until midnight. When we didn't show up, she went over to Karl's house to let his wife Karin know. Of course, they had no idea what had happened. It seems we humans always assume the worst. Needless to say, they didn't get much sleep that night.

While Karl and I worked at skinning the moose, I asked Flori to gather up some firewood. We would have to have a fire all night. I also asked him to cut a bunch of green spruce branches in case we needed a smoke signal in the morning. We had a friend in Dot Lake who had an airplane, and I thought Betty might ask him to fly over the area where we were supposed to be to try to locate us. My thinking was right on.

We built a nice fire and made ourselves as comfortable as we could. Fortunately, it wasn't too cold and it wasn't raining. The ground was damp though, so we spent the night sitting on a log. We weren't very comfortable, but we survived.

Sure enough, I think it was about 9 a.m. the next morning when we heard an airplane flying down the Tanana River. I heard his engine rev up as he turned and came up the slough. We threw a bunch of the spruce branches on the fire, and the smoke billowed up through the trees. When he went by he was about ten feet above the water. He spotted us and waved. He made two more passes, then climbed out and turned toward Dry Creek. We were relieved. Our families and friends would know that we were ok. Later the pilot told us that he saw us, and he saw the moose, but he didn't see a boat so he knew we had a problem.

A couple of hours later, a man and his young son from the farm came down the slough in a canoe. Karl had a couple of inflatable rubber rafts, and they brought one of those with them. Karl and Flori took it, while I rode out in the canoe. The pilot also had a riverboat, so we borrowed it and went back and brought our moose meat out.

When we realized our predicament, the first thing we did was to ask the Lord to help us find the boat. There are many dangers on the river. One of them is "sweepers," which are trees that hang low over the water that can capsize a boat and sink it. If it survived that type of thing it could eventually end up in the Yukon River and head on out into the Bering Sea.

If I remember correctly, this all happened on a Tuesday. The folks at the farm had an airplane and on the following Saturday one of the pilots offered to fly Karl over the Tanana River to try to find the boat. It didn't seem too promising; the boat could be almost to Fairbanks by then. Well, about two miles below the confluence of the Johnson and Tanana Rivers, they saw the boat in a little pond behind a gravel bar.

There was a narrow slip of water that went from the river to that pond. The Tanana is a fast river, so how a boat drifting downstream could make a 90-degree turn and get back into that pond was a great mystery to us. But there it was. The boat had only gone four or five miles from where it broke loose.

Our pilot friend loaned us his boat again and we put in the Tanana to retrieve our boat. I don't remember now whether our motor ran out of gas or if it just wouldn't start, but we had to tow it back upstream to the landing place. When we got to the boat we could see that everything was just as it was when it left us. Karl's camera was still sitting there on the seat, and all of my gear was also. Do you think that might have been an answer to our prayers? We certainly do!

Karl and Bob retrieve their moose, 1993*

35 The Runaway

One time Ole' Festus and I went up the old Horse Trail to the Horn Mountain area to hunt caribou. We left late and by the time we got up on top it was getting dark. I set my tent up next to the trail, staked Festus out, fed him and got some supper for myself. A light rain was coming down, and I crawled in the tent and went to sleep.

Sometime later, I woke up and heard a noise outside on the trail. I thought, "That sounds like a mule dragging his chain!" I got dressed as quickly as I could and went outside. Sure enough, Festus was gone. I had a two-foot long iron stake with a 15-foot chain and had staked him out on a slight side hill. I guess he had gotten on the high side of the stake, pulled it out, and took off.

I had a friend in Anchorage who hunted with horses every year and knew them well. I told him one time when we were visiting that I had bought a big mule and was planning to use him for hunting. He told me some of his experiences with his horses, and told me that no matter where we were Festus would always know the shortest way home. He said if my mule ever got away from me that's where he would go. Well, right now those were not comforting words.

I was imagining myself walking the five or six miles back home to get my "old buddy" and then coming back to continue my hunt. I was not about to give up that easily though, so I started calling him. "Festus, come on back Old Timer, come on back." I put a little grain in his can and started shaking it. "Hey Old Timer, come on back, I've got some grain for you." Nothing! I couldn't hear his chain dragging or any noise at all. I stood there a while longer, calling his name and shaking the grain can. Nothing.

There was a lot of night left, so I went back in the tent and lay down. I'd have to wait for daylight anyway, so I might as well get some sleep. Suddenly, I sat up—eyes wide open. I thought I had heard a noise. I grabbed my flashlight and went outside. I did hear a noise! It was getting closer. It was Festus. He had come back! I didn't know why, but there he was. That's the second time I could have almost kissed him! I gave him the grain, staked him out again in a flatter place, and went back to bed. I was very relieved, to say the least. The next day we went on and got a nice caribou and headed for home.

Festus loaded with caribou meat and antlers

Another time, Ed and I had gone up on the plateau to hunt caribou. We didn't get one on that hunt, but we always enjoyed being up there. I love that high country. The air is so fresh and pure, and the scenery so grand. If it were possible I would have a little log cabin up there!

We came down Squeaky's trail—named after a man who had a cabin a couple hundred yards up the side of the plateau. His real name was Merle. I don't know how he got that nickname, but everyone called him Squeaky and he didn't seem to mind.

We were going up that trail one year and we met him and his brother coming down with some caribou meat on packhorses. Squeaky introduced us to his brother, whose nickname was Flea.

They were both really nice guys. Squeaky still stops in to visit occasionally when he goes by our road.

The trail was wet and muddy. Just before the trail gets to Squeaky's cabin there is a steep place about fifty yards long. I should have gotten off Festus and led him down that part, but I guess I was feeling lazy that day.

About half way down, Festus slipped and fell on his right side, pinning my leg underneath him. Well, I guess you know that when you have a 1,000 pound mule lying on your leg you aren't going anywhere. Ed wasn't too far behind me, so I just waited for him. He took the reins and got Festus up, and we went on our way. If I had been alone that day, however, I think I could have slipped out of my prosthesis and gotten free. Festus might have gotten up by himself, sooner or later, but I sure was glad Ed was there.

36 Never a Dull Moment

I had a six-wheeled Max ATV. One time, Ed, Eileen and Amy came down to visit. The Max was supposed to work on land or in the water. I had been thinking of trying it out in Dry Creek. Ed said he would go, so we climbed in. We got in the creek a couple hundred yards above the bridge. We had had a lot of rain that summer, so the creek was running about three feet deep, and running fast. We got in the creek and started floating downstream fast. I immediately knew that we should not be in that creek. I could not steer the Max.

Dry Creek empties into the Johnson slough, the Johnson slough empties into the Tanana River, the Tanana River empties into the Yukon River, the Yukon River empties into the Bering Sea, and the Bering Sea runs south into the Pacific Ocean. Can you believe all of that information went through my mind in a split second? I'm sure someone would have snagged us out of the river before we ever got that far, but we had to get that thing out of the creek. We floated under the bridge at the highway. I managed to get over close to the west bank and by grabbing branches of the trees that overhung the creek; we were able to get out of the creek and out of danger. In hindsight, I think when they said you could use the machine in water; they meant still water like a lake or a pond.

Our problem was not completely solved however. The bank was too steep, and the machine wouldn't climb it. We thought about that for a few minutes and came up with an idea. Wherever I went, whether in a machine or with Festus, I always had a rope with me. We tied the rope to a tree on top of the bank, and I took several turns of the rope around the left front wheel. Ed held on to the loose end of the rope, and I got in and drove the Max. It worked! We walked that machine right up the bank and onto level ground.

I had another interesting experience with the Max. Betty and I and Billy's wife, Judy, went to Delta to get groceries. This was the summer of 1979. Billy had had a heart attack the previous winter, and didn't feel well enough to go. In those early years our roads were bad.

Our road in the early years

The road that accessed the upper Dry Creek area had been put in years before. It was just at two-track trail that had very wet, soggy areas and large rocks which made it very difficult to navigate with a pickup truck. I used that trail a lot with the Max. One thing I was not aware of was how much damage bumping over those rocks was doing to my machine.

The tub of the Max was made of molded plastic. It was a one-piece outfit, sort of like a bathtub with wheels. There were waterproof seals where the axles went through the tub. The tub material was ¼ inch thick, at least it was around the top edge, and it was all supposed to be the same thickness. However, I discovered that the bottom of the tub was only 1/16 of an inch thick.

This machine was chain driven. It had two large diameter sprockets at the rear of the machine. What I didn't realize was that every time the machine went over those big rocks, they pushed the bottom of the tub up against the sprockets, and had worn holes through the tub. The consequence of this was, of course, that it would not float. I was not aware of this problem until we got in the creek again.

The main road into the farm was muddy when it rained, but there were no big rocks. Because the old original trail was unusable a lot of the summer, Billy had cut a trail from his cabin down to the creek, a half mile or so down the creek, and then up the bank to the farm and used their road. We got back from town with the groceries. I had the Max there by the creek. There was some water in the creek, and we couldn't drive the pickup through it, but the Max would work just fine.

We were babysitting Dick and Diana's daughter, Jenny, our granddaughter, and after we got the groceries loaded up we piled in and took off. Betty was holding Jenny. We had to go around a bend of the creek. The water on the outside of the bend was about three or four feet deep, but no problem—we could float. The sand was quite loose and the machine was heavy with the groceries and all of us. I tried to keep it on the high side, but it kept sliding down towards the water. I kept moving forward but couldn't stop it from sliding sideways, and we found ourselves in the water.

We were very surprised because the tub was filling up with water. We got out as quickly as we could. Betty handed Jenny to Judy, and she took her to their cabin so Billy could watch her until we got there. Betty and I were trying to get the groceries out so they wouldn't get wet. We got the stuff out of the vehicle, but we still had some heavy bags of flour on the back of the machine. I had to get down into the water to get them.

I was handing the bags to Betty when, suddenly, my prosthesis broke. It was a temporary one. Just a socket fastened to a pylon, like an aluminum pipe about two inches in diameter with a foot bolted on the bottom end. I was trying it out to see if it fit well and didn't wear any raw spots on my leg. I was to return to Anchorage soon, and if it was ok, they would make a more permanent one for me.

They probably didn't expect that I would be doing this type of thing!

A similar experience happened once before. We were staying at the Big Timber motel in Anchorage. They fit me with one of those temporary legs. I drove over to the motel, parked my truck and started walking across the parking lot when the thing broke. As I was going down, I sort of rolled my body and hit on my right shoulder. I wasn't hurt, but it was sure embarrassing to crawl on my hands and knees over to the motel door! After this incident, they didn't let me out any more with a temporary prosthesis. I mentioned to them that if the thing broke while I was crossing a busy street, I could get run over. They agreed.

Back to my story....I managed to get back on my feet...er...uh...foot and we got the flour off the machine before it got wet. The farm folks had horses, and I had Judy ask them if they would bring a team down to pull the machine up on dry ground for me. I guess she caused some excitement when she told them of our problem and mentioned that I had broken my leg. I had another prosthesis at the cabin, and Betty walked back and got it for me so I was mobile again.

The guys came with the horses and pulled my machine back up out of the water. I couldn't get the engine started because it had gotten wet. Billy was a good mechanic and he came over and got it going. We loaded the groceries up again and took them right to their cabin door. It was quite an ordeal, but it all worked out fine in the end.

37 The Apprentice

Every year when moose season came around, I had the decision to make about where to hunt. There were several good places I could go, but I had to decide which one I thought would give me the best chance to get a moose. There is a small gravel pit a couple miles down the road, and one morning I decided to go there. Sometimes the moose would come down out of the hills and cross that area on their way to the river.

I got up on a high place where I had good visibility. There was a light wind blowing and rustling the leaves on the brush, which made it difficult to hear. I'd been there an hour or so when I thought I heard a bull making his grunting sound. I listened closely and, sure enough, it was a bull. He was moving away from me. I couldn't see him, but there was a large gravel pit just a couple hundred yards in the direction he was going.

I stood there debating with myself as to whether I should stay where I was, or go down to the other gravel pit. I decided to go. I hopped in the truck and drove down there. I pulled into the trees and parked. I happened to look in my rearview mirror, and there he was on the far side of the gravel pit, heading for the river. He was going pretty fast and I needed to get him before he crossed the highway, because on the north side of the road the land dropped off into the thick brush and I wouldn't get another chance at him.

I grabbed my rifle, jumped out of the truck and shot, but I thought I missed him. He turned and headed back in the direction he came from, went about 30 feet, turned around again, and headed back towards the road. I shot again and he went down. When we got him skinned out I discovered that I had hit him both times. The first shot hit four or five inches below the top of his back. It missed his backbone and the lung and went right on through. I think he would have survived that shot.

I was only three miles from home, so I went back to the cabin and got Betty, and she came and helped me get him skinned out and quartered. We trimmed all of the meat off the ribs, cut the tenderloins and the backstrap out, and left the rib cage there. The birds and mice would have a little snack too. We didn't have to pack the meat because I was able to back the truck right up to the spot and load it. It was a whole lot easier than some other times.

On the way home we met some folks who had just moved to the farm from Minnesota. We both stopped, and he was all excited about me getting a moose. It was only about a 45" rack, but a lot of meat, a nice bull. He said that he would sure like to get one. They were Ron and Marge. They had two daughters, Joan and Jackie, and a son, Jason. They were really nice folks and we became good friends. Ron would get a very nice bull, but more about that later.

Sometime later, Jason asked if he could go on my trapline with me, and I said I'd be glad to have him along. He did go with me and trapped with me for about seven years. He was a quick learner, and was soon setting traps and catching fur. I showed him how to make trail sets and blind sets. We didn't use any bait for those and they were very effective for that reason. The farm had a place across the road where they dumped the innards and bones of critters they butchered, and it was a great place to catch coyotes and fox. They had trails from the thick woods to those piles. I showed him how to cut the track out with a knife and slide a trap under it so the pan was right in the track, then sprinkle a little snow on the trap to hide it. When the snow gets deep the animals walk in the same tracks so it's a very successful method.

After Billy had his heart attack, he had to quit the trapline. I trapped alone then for a lot of years. Cutting trail alone was a lot slower. I was trying to get from the East Fork to Plateau Lake. I got to within a quarter mile of dropping down into the flats west of the lake, and from there to the lake it was small willow brush, and I wouldn't have to do any cutting on that part.

I came home and told Betty about it and asked her if she wanted to go with me the next day. She said she'd like to do that. I told her that I was sure that we could make it all the way to the lake. We went up the next day and we did get to the lake.

Lunchtime on Plateau Lake

We built a fire and had a nice lunch. It was a beautiful day and we were really enjoying it. The trail came about 50 yards down a hill before we got to the flats, and the last 20 feet or so dropped off a little steeper.

In this country, once you make a trail in the snow it freezes hard and makes a good trail. Usually though, it has to set overnight to do that. The snow was deep, and the trail was fresh and still soft. We left the lake and headed home. We got to the hill and I hit the throttle to get a good start up the hill. We got about 20 feet and got bogged down in the deep snow, I bounced the machine up and down a few times to pack the snow, and told Betty to push on the sled. We got bogged down again.

I unhooked the sled, turned the snow machine around and went back down. I got a good start, hit the hill again and got to the top. I had some 1/4" nylon rope with me. I went down, tied the rope to the sled, went back up and tied it to the snow machine. With Betty pushing the sled, we were able to get it up the hill just fine. "All in a day's work!" as the old saying goes.

In all of this trail cutting, my plan was to get from the East Fork to Plateau Lake, and then on over to upper Sears Creek. My trapline already went a few miles up Sears Creek and I wanted to connect with it. That way I wouldn't have to backtrack; I could make a circle all the way around and back to the cabin. I mentioned that to Jason when he started trapping with me, and every time we went up there we cut more trail from Plateau Lake. We eventually got to Sears Creek, and it all worked out as planned.

A sunny day on the trapline. My sled with all my essentials *

Our trail cutting never ended because there was always another valley to check out, or another ridge to get over in our quest for new trapping ground. Jason was a hard working young man, and we accomplished most of our goals and had fun as well.

My plan for Jason was to help him notice and enjoy the beauty of the land, as well as teach him how to set traps. There was one particular spot on our trail just east of Plateau Lake that he liked a lot. He even said it was his most favorite spot on the whole trail. It was on the side of a hill and had a great view to the east.

Setting a trap at Plateau Lake *

We could see the cut banks along which the Tanana River flowed, and the hills and valleys beyond. It usually worked out that we got there around noontime, so we took a break and had lunch. It was the highlight of our day.

Back in Michigan I had hunted deer for a few years with my dad, and one thing we always tried to do was get together around noon, build a fire, and toast our sandwiches. I'll tell you right now that a warm toasted sandwich out there in the cold and snow sure tastes a lot better than a cold soggy one. That's what Jason and I did too. We had toasted sandwiches, hot coffee and whatever else we could find in our sack.

That high country is so beautiful. Sometimes on bright sunny days we would shut our snow machines off and just sit there and take it all in.

*Enjoying the beauty and the quiet with Plateau Lake in the background ***

There was always a place on the creek where we could get a nice cold drink of water too, whenever we needed one. Sometimes there would be an open place, and sometimes we would go along until we heard the water gurgling underneath the ice. The ice was pretty thin there, and easy to break a hole through.

Finishing a day on the trapline *

Another trick I learned from my dad was how to build a fire when the woods were saturated with several days of rain. Dad and I were out hunting deer one time in just such conditions. It was getting close to noon so I was trying to start a fire. Everything, and I mean everything, was wet. Even the small twigs on the trunk of the trees were saturated.

Well, my dad came along, and I told him that I was having trouble getting a fire going because everything was so wet. He said, "I'll show you how to do that!" I already had a lot of twigs and small sticks so he got a piece of birch bark, then went over to a spruce tree and with his knife cut off some pitch balls. When a spruce tree gets damaged, the sap leaks out and then hardens. He laid four or five of those pitch balls on the bark and lit them. As they burned, they melted and spread out. He laid some twigs and small sticks on it, and in just a few minutes we had a good fire going.

In my hunting equipment, and in my trapping sled, I always have some of those pitch balls with me. You can light them with a match, and they burn hot and long enough to dry the sticks out so they'll burn. It's a good idea to always have some of them with you when out in the "wilds." You never know when you'll need a quick fire. You can find them on most any spruce tree. They are free and they really work.

38 Ron's First Moose

Another moose season rolled around. Jason's dad, Ron, came over one day and told me that he had heard of a good place where he might get a moose but he didn't know how to get there. He described it and I told him I knew the place and I agreed to take him. We got there around noon or so. It was a place that had two small ponds, and the trees were sparse.

We picked out a spot where we had good visibility of the whole area and got comfortable. From where we sat it was about 150 yards to the far side of the clearing. A light rain was falling, and the air was cooling off. We decided that a small fire would feel good, gathered up some small sticks, and built a fire between us. It did feel good.

We sat there until around 3:00 p.m. but hadn't seen any moose. Our fire was dying down, and we were getting chilly. I mentioned to Ron that late afternoon was a good time to start seeing moose, and maybe we should get some more firewood so we wouldn't be moving around later and maybe spook a bull. He thought that was a good idea.

We didn't have a saw with us, so we found some smaller dry wood and were whacking it over a log to break it into smaller pieces. We were making a lot of noise. Suddenly Ron said, "Listen!" We heard a bull somewhere beyond the other side of the clearing and it sounded like he was coming our way. He was doing his grunts and was coming fast.

Anyone not familiar with moose might think it strange that they would come while we were making so much noise. When bull moose are in the rut (the mating season) and they hear sounds of brush cracking, they think it's another bull. Sometimes the bulls will walk through the woods whacking their antlers on trees and brush looking for a fight, and if there are any other bulls that hear it, they will come running. Some hunters walk through the woods with small antlers or a dried shoulder blade, whacking them on the brush, and can call a bull in.

In just a few seconds the bull came into sight on the far side of the clearing. Ron would do the shooting. He knelt down and leaned his arm against a tree preparing to shoot. About that time the bull turned and was coming straight towards us. I told Ron not to shoot yet because he might turn sideways, and he could get a better shot. Ron said ok, he was just getting ready. We had enough time and daylight. The area was wide open and there was no way that bull was going to get away from us!

The sight of that big bull coming towards us like that was awesome. It really gets your heart pumping. He came another 50 yards or so, turned broadside to us and stopped. He just stood there looking right at us. Ron squeezed the trigger, and his 7 mm magnum roared. That bull reared up on his hind legs and fell over backwards, flat on his back! He couldn't have been in a better position for skinning. All we had to do was tie a rope on one hind leg, run the rope around a tree and pull his leg up to where we could get at him, and tie the rope off.

We spent a few minutes admiring him: lots of meat, a nice rack, a good one-shot kill, and a slap on the back for Ron. He said he would go back to the farm and get some horses to pack the meat out. As I was skinning away, the thought came to me that I didn't have to pack any of this moose out on my back: a very good feeling! Ron came back with his son Jason, another guy, and three horses. They all pitched in and we finished butchering the moose and loaded him on the horses. Each horse had all he could carry, and with that big 50" rack on top of one of them, it was very impressive. Ron was one happy guy. His first moose! I don't know how long he kept that smile on his face, but the last time I saw him, he was still grinning from ear to ear. That scene would have made a great picture, but no one had a camera with them!

39 A Little More Horsepower?

Billy had recovered quite well from his heart attack and was thinking about hunting again. The place he wanted to go was about 10 miles east of Dot Lake and down along the Tanana River. He had a boat and a 9½ horsepower motor that we took along with us. His thinking was that if we shot something on the far bank of the river we could use the boat to retrieve it.

I took my track machine to use between where we had to leave our vehicles and the river. That way, Billy wouldn't have to do much walking so it would be easier on him. In joking, he often referred to himself as a "poor old heart attack victim," sort of letting us know we should make things as easy for him as we could. We all got many laughs over that.

Judy and Billy with the Kidd ATV, Fall 1979

Judy came along too. We got down to the river and we all picked out a spot to sit down and watch. A short time later, we saw a young bull moose on the far side of a gravel bar near the north bank of the river. We watched him for a while. He was just moseying along heading downstream. Billy decided he didn't want to shoot him.

By then the bull was out of sight. I decided to go farther downstream, and if he showed up, I was going to shoot him. I was hungry for some fresh meat! The gravel bar ran about 200 yards downstream. I went almost to the end of it, found a good place to sit, and got ready to shoot.

I don't remember how long it was until the bull showed up, maybe half an hour. He was still on the far side of the gravel bar and all I could see was his head and neck. A few minutes later he walked up on the bar to where I could see his front shoulder. I put the crosshairs of my scope just behind the shoulder and shot. He dropped out of sight. I was sure that my shot was good and that he was down. Billy and Judy came over. There was a little hill just beyond where we were, and Billy climbed up on it and said, "Yup, he's down, but he's in two feet of water."

I couldn't see beyond the gravel bar from where I was, but there was a strip of water 30 or 40 yards wide between the gravel bar and the north bank of the river. We went back to the track machine, then back to our vehicles, and loaded the boat on the track machine. I got a come-along and some ¼" cable that I had in my truck, and we went over to the moose.

Sure enough, he was about 25 yards out in two feet of water. Billy had his boots on, so he went out and hooked the cable to the moose. We tied the come-along to a tree on the riverbank and winched the moose up on the gravel bar where we could work on him.

In a situation like this, if there were plenty of daylight left, we would have made two trips out with the meat. However, it was getting dark and we had been hearing noises back in the brush. Of course, the first thing you think about in that situation is "grizzly bear" which is a very real possibility!

Getting the moose up where we could work on him

We didn't want to take a chance on leaving any of the meat, and we definitely did not want to make another trip in the dark. By the time we got the moose skinned and butchered it was nearly dark. We took the time to trim the meat off the ribs, and then cut the backstraps and tenderloins out. We left the rib cage and backbone there to save room in the boat, and it was time to get out of there!

We got everything loaded in the boat. Billy started the motor and we headed out into the river. We got right out into the middle of the river and the motor died. Not good! There we were, floating backward down the river, in the dark!

There are many dangers on the river including the sweepers, as I have already mentioned, which could capsize the boat and dump us out into the cold water. The boat was heavily loaded and sitting very low in the water, and it wouldn't take much to swamp it. A picture flashed through my mind of the next day's Fairbanks Daily News-Miner, "Three Moose Hunters Drown in the Tanana River!"

Billy was frantically pulling the starting rope trying to get the motor started, and I was concerned that he might have another heart attack. He had a piece of board in the boat, and I used that to get us back over to the gravel bar. Billy discovered that he had forgotten to open the valve on the fuel line from the gas can. He got the motor started, and we were on our way again.

We got out in the middle of the river and that little motor was chugging along trying to move the heavy load. I was in the bow of the boat. We only had about 3 inches of freeboard (a Navy term for the distance from the surface of the water to the main deck of a ship or top edge of the boat) and the water was splashing in.

I called to Billy to slow down or he was going to swamp us! He replied that he couldn't slow down because we were already going backwards. There was a big rock sticking up out of the water to our left. I shined my flashlight on it. We really were going backwards. Billy then began to ease the boat over towards the south bank where the current was slower, and we began to make some headway. Even so, it took us 20 minutes or so to get up to where our track machine was.

All was well! We got our moose out, we didn't have any problem with bears, and we were back on solid ground again. Another successful hunt! Prior to this experience, Billy was always bragging about his 9½ horsepower motor and what it could do. A few days later we were sitting around talking about the hunt. I said to him, "Billy, I've got a question for you. Tell me the truth now! Don't you think that a little more horsepower would have been good out there on the river?" He smiled and said, "Yeah...probably." We all had a good laugh!

40 The Disappearing Moose

One hunting season Festus and I were on our way up the plateau to see if we could find a moose. We were above the tree line and I reined him up to look around. I looked over toward Dry Lake. On the north side there is an old tractor trail that leads to the Johnson Slough. I saw a moose heading for that trail. It was a cow, but I decided to check it out. When we got over there I staked Festus out in a grassy area. I thought if I was careful and quiet I might get a look at the moose, or maybe see another one.

I walked back in there a half mile or so and found a good place to sit and watch. I hadn't seen any moose, but I had been very quiet and was sure I hadn't spooked anything. It was already late afternoon, so I was hoping something would show up soon. Then I heard a cow moose off in the distance, and she was coming my way. The brush was quite thick and I couldn't see very far, but she was getting close. She was bawling constantly. Then I noticed the tops of some tall willows whipping back and forth, so I guessed that there was more than one moose there.

Suddenly, a young bull came out of the brush about 25 yards away, moving to my right. Before I could shoot, he turned and walked straight away from me. Well, I didn't want to shoot him in the rump so I waited. Then he disappeared. Just like that, he was gone. I never saw the cow, but she went on in the same direction as the bull. I could hear her for a long time, still moving away from me. It was dark by this time so I walked out, and Festus and I came home. I was a little disappointed, but that's the way hunting is.

I was still wondering how that bull disappeared like he did, so the next morning I went back over there. I discovered a turned up root system about seven feet high. The moose had gotten behind that and disappeared. About a week later, Betty and I were outside the cabin and heard a cow moose down by the creek. She was bawling away, hoping for a bull to come along. I wondered if it was the same one I had heard over at Dry Lake. We walked out to the creek to have a look. There she was about 50 yards downstream.

She had a spring calf, and two yearling bulls with her. They must have been her calves from the previous year. They both had identical antlers, about 24" wide. They looked just like the one I had seen at Dry Lake. The only problem now was that moose season was closed. Well, maybe they would still be around next year, if they survived the wolves and the bears.

41 The Birthday Moose

In September of 1979, Betty made a trip back to Michigan. Her parents' 50th wedding anniversary was the 18th of September, and Betty's birthday was the 19th, so they were going to celebrate together. We had also bought a clock for them shaped like the State of Alaska, and she wanted to give it to them in person.

In those years, moose season stayed open until September 20th, instead of closing on the 15th. I really liked that because I believe those last five days were better hunting than the first fifteen days. It was closer to the mating season, and the bulls moved around more.

I hadn't gotten my moose yet, so Festus and I went up on the plateau on the 18th to see if we could find one. There is a large valley just up over the ridge from our cabin, and that's where we went. It was late afternoon by the time we got there, so I staked Festus out, fed him his grain, and set up camp. I had some supper and sat on a rock overlooking the valley for a while. It was a couple hundred yards down to the bottom of the valley, where a small creek ran through.

It was a nice day, and there was no indication that the next day, the 19th, would be any different. Ha! Alaska was being Alaska again: unpredictable! I woke up the next morning to find the whole area socked in with fog. You have to be flexible when you live in Alaska. That's what I keep telling Betty, anyway!

No problem, I gave Festus his grain and had some breakfast. When we were up in that high country, I gave him grain morning and night. He could find some grass and other green stuff here and there, but it wasn't like when he was home and had lots of hay to eat. About ten o'clock the fog started to lift. So I got my rifle and binoculars, and sat back down for a while. The fog finally cleared away, and that rock was getting tired of me sitting on it, so I got up to stretch and look around.

When I'm hunting, the main thing I look for is a difference in color — something that doesn't blend in with the surrounding vegetation. Down in the valley to the north, something caught my eye. I focused on it for a minute, and it moved a little. I looked at it through my binoculars, and it was a bull moose — a big one! I guessed that his antler spread was at least 60", maybe more. Things were looking good! He was feeding about 500 yards away and was working slowly my way.

The problem was, when he got closer to the bottom of the hill I was on I wouldn't be able to see him anymore. It would have been a long shot, and my .300 Winchester Magnum would probably have done the job at 500 yards, but I saw no reason to be in a rush and decided to wait him out. He did get out of sight, but I continued to watch, hoping he would get out to where I could see him again. If he did show up again, it would be a more sure shot. I could already see those big antlers hanging over my cabin door.

Just then I caught a movement out of the corner of my eye to my left. There was another bull coming up the hill. He was a smaller one and had already seen me, wheeled around, and was headed back downhill. I was beginning to get frustrated. All these bull moose running around, and I hadn't had a chance at one yet.

I looked over to see if I could see the big one, and he still hadn't showed up. I looked a little farther to my left, down through an opening in the trees, and down in the valley stood another bull. He was just standing there. I guessed that he was watching those other bulls. I quickly put the crosshairs of my scope behind his shoulder and squeezed the trigger.

He just stood there. I know my rifle, and where it shoots, and I was sure that I had hit him. However, the way things had been going for me the last half hour or so, I decided to shoot again. He just stood there, but a few seconds later he began to cough and blow out steam, and then he dropped right where he stood. I saddled Festus up, put the panniers on the saddle, and went down to the moose. He had about a 45" rack, and a large body — a lot of meat on this guy. I checked for bullet holes, and there were two holes about 3" apart, both of them through the lungs.

Well, I had my work cut out for me. I'm not too good at guessing weight out in the field, but I think my moose weighed close to a thousand pounds, maybe more. My plan was to get him skinned out, cut up and packed up to my campsite, and then pack him home the next day. It would take two trips, and I would have to walk, but I wouldn't have to pack any meat out on my back. A good feeling indeed.

I laid out a plastic tarp that I had brought along to lay the meat on to keep it clean, and went to work on him. I skinned out one side so I could cut the front and hindquarters off, then rolled him over, skinned out the other side, and removed the other two quarters. I rolled the carcass up on its back, slit it open, and rolled the innards out. I cut the tenderloins out, cut the back straps off and trimmed the rest of the meat off the ribs. That saved some weight, and a lot of bulk. No use packing all that bone out! I trimmed the meat off the pelvic bone and the neck. When I was finished with all of that, I put the meat in game bags.

I used my meat saw to cut the top of the skull off with the antlers. According to Alaska game regulations, the antlers have to come out with the last load of meat, so I would have to leave them for the second load. I rolled the hide up — that would come out with the last load also. Well, all that was left to do was get the meat loaded on Festus.

The muskeg was a foot deep and difficult to move around in. The only way I could get the meat in the panniers was to lay it up on the saddle, pull the pannier open with my left hand, and let the meat slide down into it. The front quarters probably weighed 75 or 80 pounds, and the hindquarters close to 100 pounds, so it was a difficult job. To make matters worse, I guess Festus was feeling a little lazy because when I approached him with a big piece of meat, he started sidestepping away from me! He kept doing his little dance, with me following him around trying to load the meat. I sure didn't feel like kissing him that day! I felt more like whopping him over the head with a tree limb!

I finally won out and got a load on him. I decided after all of that, I wasn't going to unpack that load until I got home, so we headed out. It got dark before we got back to the cabin, but we made it ok. We went back the next day and got the rest of the meat, hide, and antlers. I was able to get my tent on the load too.

I hung the meat to let it age a little. A few days later I took most of it into Delta to the freezer. In those days, the only phones that were available to us in Delta were pay phones. We had to go to the bank and get some quarters. Then we usually went over to the Bay Hotel. It was a good place to get something to eat, and it was a convenient place to use the phone. I wanted to call Betty and tell her that I had gotten her a present for her birthday — close to 400 pounds of moose meat. She was happy about that!

Despite all of the work, we were very thankful to have all that good meat. It was hard work for old Festus and me, but it was worth it. I don't know how Festus felt about it, but I gave him extra grain every day for the next week, so I think he was a happy old mule. I sure couldn't have done it without him.

42 Goodbye Old Friend

Caribou hunting season rolled around again. Bob had a nephew who had never been hunting, and he asked me if I would take him up on Macomb Plateau to try and get a caribou. I agreed, so we went up. I gave him some instructions, and found a good spot for him to sit and watch. I explained how to tell a bull caribou from a cow. This was necessary because both bulls and cows have antlers. A cow has much smaller antlers than a bull, but a young bull can look very similar to a cow, and one has to be very careful. A large, older bull has large antlers, and cannot be mistaken for a cow.

Festus and I went on over a hill a little distance away so we wouldn't interfere with his hunt. A short time later I heard him shoot. We went over and he had a nice caribou. He was a happy young man. We processed the caribou and loaded him on Festus. This was just a one-day hunt, so I didn't have my camp. It was a small caribou so I could ride out instead of walking. Lance had to walk, but he was young, so no problem.

All had gone well up until now, but Festus was acting strange. He was wandering, like he wasn't sure which way to go. He knew the trail well, but one time he left it and headed for the edge where the land dropped off sharply several hundred feet down to upper Dry Creek. He had never acted like this before, so I knew there was something very wrong with the old timer. We got down ok, and back to the corral where I gave him some grain and hay.

The next day I fed him as usual in the morning. He ate his grain and a little hay, and later I saw him rolling around on the ground. Sometimes horses and mules get a "twisted gut" and by rolling around they can straighten it out. At least that was my understanding at the time, from what someone had told me. They also said that sometimes walking them would help. I put a halter on him and led him a ways down our road. He didn't want to go. He would take a few steps and stop. I finally led him back to the corral.

I had to go to Delta that day, but I spent a little time talking to him, scratching his big ears and rubbing his neck. I told him, "I've got to go to Delta, old timer, but I'll be back in a couple of hours." I was very concerned about him because he was just standing there with his head down and his tongue hanging out. I've always regretted that I didn't stay with him, instead of going to town.

When I got back from Delta, I looked out toward the corral but couldn't see him. I went right over there where I found him lying on the ground, dead! It was a very sad day for me! My neighbors had a bulldozer, and I asked them if they would come over and dig a hole so I could bury him. They did, and he is buried right there in his corral.

Sometimes, I sit here looking out the window, drinking a cup of coffee, and in my mind's eye I can see Festus standing by his grain box waiting for me to come out and feed him. My mind begins to wander into the past and I remember some of the adventures that he and I had.

I only had him seven years, but those seven years were full of good and exciting times. Without Festus, I could never have done all the hunting I did. I could saddle him up, load my camp and my rifle, and ride all the way to my caribou camp. Festus was a faithful old friend, a big and powerful mule, but as it is with all flesh, he got to the place where he just couldn't go any farther. I still miss him.

43 Building My New Flintlocks

After Festus died I took his shed down and built a storage building closer to the cabin. I also converted the pole barn into a workshop. I put windows all across the west end and built my workbench there. I had been thinking of building another flintlock rifle—a larger caliber for hunting in grizzly country. I decided on a .69 cal. rifle with a 48" octagon to round, tapered and flared barrel.

I also built a .69 cal. pistol to go with it, in case I needed a quick second shot! The rifle barrel was 1¼ inch at the breech. It was octagon from the breech 16 inches, then round from there and tapered and flared to the muzzle. The pistol barrel was 10 inches long, 1⅛ inches at the breech, octagon 4-¼ inches, then round and tapered and flared to 1 inch at the muzzle. They both have curly maple stocks. I have hunted with them, but have not had a chance at a moose yet. I use round balls only. They weigh 450 grains, and I think they would do a good job on a moose. I still have my .300 Winchester, but I sure do like to hunt with my muzzleloader. Maybe one day I'll get a moose with it.

.69 Cal. Flintlock Rifle

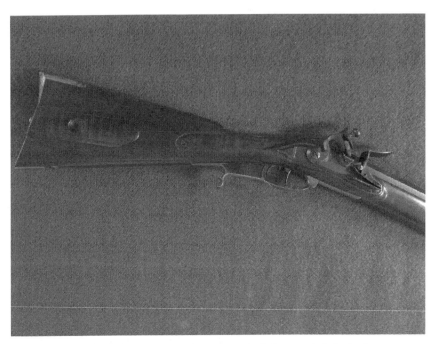

Note the wooden patch box cover and close-up of the lock

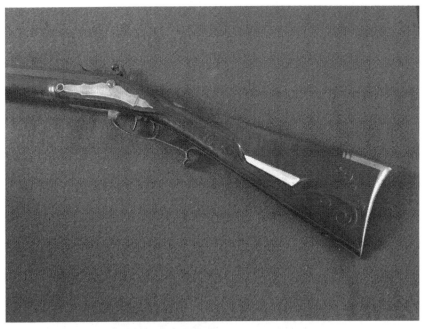

Cheek piece featuring fossilized Mastodon Ivory

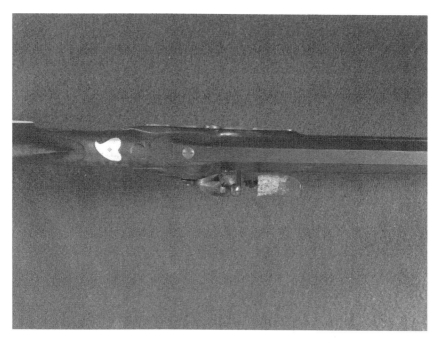

Signature 'Weeping Heart'

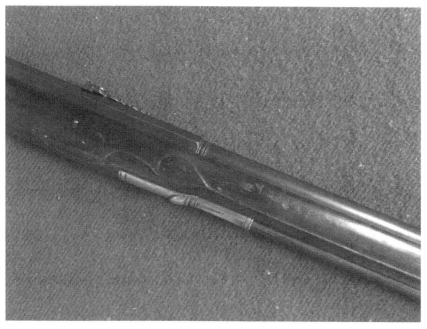

Transition from octagon barrel to round

Bob with .69 cal. Flintlock Rifle, September 1990

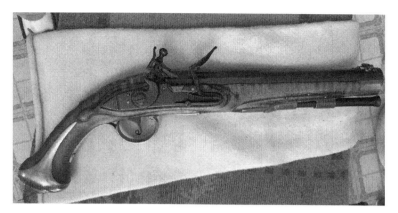

.69 Caliber Flintlock Pistol

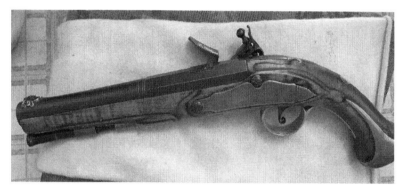

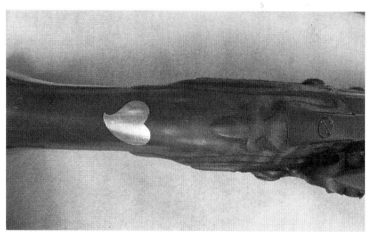

Signature 'Weeping Heart' on Pistol

'Grotesque Mask' front sight on pistol—the nose is the sight blade.

Bob in his workshop, after he moved it to the garage

*Bob in full muzzle loading costume ***

I don't get around in the woods too well anymore, but I keep thinking that after being here 40 years, I should be able to shoot a moose right off my front deck. I could sit out there in my comfortable chair, have coffee and cookies, and wait for him to show up...during hunting season, that is! We have had bull moose in our yard many times, before and after hunting season. Seems to me like I should be able to do that, but time will tell.

One year, Ed and T.J. came down to their cabin across the creek to hunt moose. Down the highway a few miles is a short stretch of the old Alaska Highway that was no longer used after they straightened and relocated it. They were hunting there. Late one afternoon a large bull moose showed up on his way to the river. He was approximately 300 yards from T.J. when he saw it. He shot, and the bull turned and headed back the way he had come from. They found a blood trail where he crossed the highway. He was bleeding enough to follow him across the road, but it was very difficult tracking after he got in the brush.

In a situation like that you need all the help you can get, so they came and got me. Eileen and Betty also went along. The women stayed on the road so if the bull went back across the road they could let us know. Later, Eileen told us that she heard something, or someone, walking in water. We didn't hear it, and we were not in the water, so it must have been the bull. Anyway, we didn't get him.

T.J. was very disappointed. He said that it was the biggest bull he had ever seen, live or even in pictures. Ed said, after that when they saw a picture of a bull moose, they asked T.J if the one he shot at was that big. He always answered, "He was bigger than that!" He must have been a really big one. It sure was too bad we couldn't find him, but I believe he survived that shot. T.J. did get a nice bull another year though, and he felt good about that.

44 Bear Encounters

I guess I've mentioned that we have had many bears in our yard down through the years. In 1975, while I was up on the slope working, a bear came in and was tramping around in our garden. Before I left, I showed Betty how to operate one of my rifles, a 30-30 lever action Winchester, just in case that happened. But I also told her not to shoot a bear unless it was a life or death situation.

When she discovered the bear in the garden, Betty got the rifle and went outside. She was pretty upset because he was walking all over her vegetable plants. The kids were urging her to shoot the bear, especially Brian I guess, but she told them that I had told her not to shoot unless she really had to. They went back in the cabin and watched the bear out the window. After a while he left and really didn't do that much damage.

One time I was working on my rifle out in my workshop. It was early, around 6 am. I just happened to look out towards the cabin and saw a black bear standing up on his hind legs trying to see in the window. He stood there for a couple minutes then dropped down on all fours and disappeared around the corner of the cabin. I kept watching and saw him dragging the garbage bag over behind the woodpile.

I came up quietly, got my .44 out just in case, and peeked around the woodpile. He was sitting there on his rump with his head in the garbage bag. There was no garbage in it, only cans, but he was really trying to find something to eat in there. I stepped around the woodpile. He heard me and looked straight at me. I jumped and hollered, "Get out of here!" He jumped up and hightailed it into the woods as fast as he could go.

After that episode, we got a metal garbage can. We never put anything in it but empty cans, but the smell of what was in them was still there. One morning, about 2:00 a.m., I heard the garbage can fall over. I got up and looked out the window and saw a young grizzly. I got our camera and took a picture of him through the window. I took my .44 just in case, stepped out the door and looked around the corner of the cabin. He was still there so I took another picture. He heard the noise and looked at me. I hollered, "Get out of here!" and he took off down the driveway like a streak.

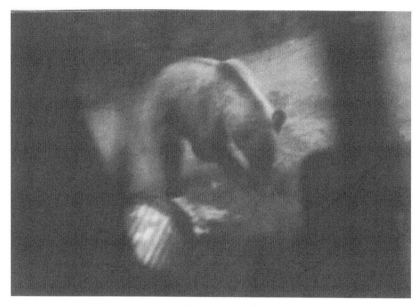

Young grizzly in our garbage can

Another time we had a cinnamon bear hanging around. He hung around for several days. He wasn't bothering anything so I didn't pay much attention to him. Betty wanted me to shoot him, but I wasn't interested in that at all. "Do you know how much work it is, skinning out a bear?" I asked. Bear meat is ok, but if there is almost any other kind of meat around, I'll take it instead. Well, he kept hanging around and became a nuisance so I decided to run him off. One day our dog, Grey Bear, was out in his doghouse and the bear was walking around, I guess trying to intimidate him. I got my rifle and shot at a tree close to him, and blew some bark off at him. He went out of there in a hurry and we never saw him again.

One day, a black bear came into the yard, and our dog put him up a tree out by the creek. I told the dog to stay, and went to get my camera. While I was gone the dog left, so the bear left. Bad dog!

Another time a black bear came in by my workshop and Grey Bear saw it. He took off after him. I don't know how far he chased that bear, but he was gone about a half hour. Well, as I have mentioned, we have had lots of bears, and always before, I just hollered at them and they hightailed it out of here.

A few years ago we had a bear experience that was a little different. About 5:30 one afternoon, Betty was cooking supper. She had the kitchen window open. I was reading and our dog started barking. I could tell by his bark that it was more serious than someone driving in the yard. I was on my way out to see what was going on, and just as I took hold of the door knob, our dog Blue ran past the door with a grizzly bear right behind him Our door opens outward, and I was sure glad that I didn't open it a few seconds sooner or we might have had them both in the cabin with us. Wouldn't that have been interesting?

I went out on the deck to see where they went. I wasn't concerned about Blue because he can really run fast, and I didn't think that bear had any chance of having him for supper. Betty yelled that the bear was looking in the window. I didn't know which window but I looked down the west side of the cabin and didn't see either of them. I didn't see Blue anywhere, but Betty said that he had gotten to the door and wanted in. She let him in.

The bear had been right behind the dog, but when he got to the kitchen window he must have smelled the food odors coming out. Betty said the bear reared up on his hind legs and started whacking the window trying to break it out. He pushed a front foot through the window, and knocked the screen out and almost hit Betty in the face. She started yelling, "Get out of here!" and stomping her foot. I went back in the cabin, and I could see that this bear was not about to leave on his own.

We hadn't had any bears around for a while, and I had become a little careless. My shotgun was in the closet and it was unloaded. I got it out and loaded several 12-gauge slugs in it. The bear was still whacking that window trying to break it out. I stepped out the door and went to the end of the deck. The bear saw me and turned toward me. I had my gun up, and when I saw one of his eyes in my sights I pulled the trigger. He dropped right where he stood; he never knew what hit him. The distance from where I stood to the bear was seven feet.

When he turned toward me, I wasn't sure if he was going to charge me or turn and run away, but I couldn't take any chances. If his intention was to charge, one jump and he would have been on me, and I might not have had a chance to shoot. Well, this all happened in a lot less time than it has taken me to write about it. I don't think the whole scenario lasted more than two or three minutes.

Betty's foot was so sore from stomping the floor that she could hardly walk on it the rest of the day. I was able to repair the window with parts that I robbed from another window that we rarely opened anyway. We ate a quick supper, and I went to work on the bear. I took the hide and the skull to Fish and Game the next day to have them sealed. This happened on May 16th and grizzly season was open, so I could keep the hide and skull, and the meat if I wanted it.

If hunting season had not been open, it still would have been legal for me to shoot him in defense of life or property. But I would have been responsible to skin it out and take the hide and skull to Fish and Game for sealing, and I would have had to turn everything over to them. A friend wanted the meat so I gave it to him. I salted the hide real well, and tacked it up on the side of my garage to let it dry out.

Our daughter, Janet, came to visit the next summer and she helped me get it nailed up on the cabin wall. We put it right next to the window that he was trying to get in. I boiled the skull so I could get the meat off, and planned to bleach it out and put it up on a shelf in my garage next to my other one. After it boiled long enough, I started scraping the flesh off of it, and the skull came apart in fifteen pieces (I counted them). The 12-gauge slug had shattered it.

Whenever I walked out to get the mail, or just took a walk in the woods, that shotgun was with me. I believe that at close range, up to 25 yards or so, a 12-gauge shotgun with slugs is good bear protection.

45 "I Can't Tell Yet!"

One time Bob came down with a couple of his horses and we went caribou hunting. He would be the shooter, and I was going to be his helper. This would be another one-day hunt.

We got up on top of the plateau and were riding along slowly looking for caribou. We were on Berry Creek Ridge, and were close to the west end of it when we looked behind us and saw a lone caribou coming toward us. He was still about 500 yards away and the antlers were pretty small so we couldn't tell if it was a cow or a bull.

We had dismounted and Bob was getting ready to shoot. I was watching the caribou through my binoculars. Bob said, "Is it a bull?" and I said, "I can't tell yet." He was looking for meat, not a trophy, so if it was a bull, no matter how small, he was going to take it. "Is it a bull?" he asked again. "I can't tell yet, Bob," I answered.

The caribou was coming straight towards us. The only way to positively identify a young bull is to see the penis sheath, and you can only see that by looking at the side of the animal. It is very prominent from a side view, but he was still coming straight at us. "Is it a bull?" Bob asked. Again I said, "I can't tell yet, Bob!" Then, I think he saw us, and turned and started running broadside to us toward the top of the ridge. I said, "It's a bull, Bob!" He shot, and the caribou bit the dust, so to speak! Another successful hunt

Another humorous event, at least to Betty and me, took place while caribou hunting when the kids were with us. We had long since tired of five bodies in a two-man tent, so we bought the kids some tube tents. They were not real tents because they were open on both ends. They just provided a shelter over the top. Our camp was located on sloping ground. During the night it rained really hard. We heard some scuffling around and talking outside. The tents kept them from getting rained on from above, but the water was running right through them. We finished out the night with five bodies in our two-man tent...three of them very wet.

46 Betty Learns to Mush

The term "mushing dogs" comes from the French Canadian term "Marche' On." Alaskans just simplified it to "Mush." I mentioned once that we had gotten a couple of puppies from some friends in Dot Lake. The first year we had them, "Wolf" disappeared. The next year, "Bear" disappeared. The wolves came through quite often in those early years, so we thought they had gotten them. We all felt bad about that, and we missed them.

One day when Betty and I were in Delta we saw a note on a bulletin board that some folks had a few puppies to give away. We went to see them and got two males. They would be large dogs; they had some malamute and husky blood.

When we got home it was dark. We carried some groceries to the cabin, and the kids met us at the door to take them. The next trip we brought the two puppies and when they opened the door we shoved the dogs at them. They were very surprised and happy. We named one "Tim" because he acted very timid until he got to know us, and the other "Yukon," which just sounded like a good Alaska/Canada name.

One day, Tim proved that he was anything but timid. I was sitting in our cabin drinking a cup of coffee and reading when Tim started to bark. He was standing by the wood shed and looking into the woods. I went out to take a look, and a saw a black bear about fifteen feet up in a birch tree. I got my shotgun and Tim and I went into the woods. I shot the bear, and as soon as it hit the ground Tim was on him, snarling and growling. The bear was dead, but I guess Tim wanted to be sure.

215

The next day I took the hide and skull into Fish & Game in Delta to get them sealed. Later I got a report in the mail from F&G and they told me that the bear was seven years old. F&G don't do that anymore. That's too bad, because it was really nice to know that info. We needed the meat, but we couldn't eat it. It was very bitter. This happened on the 10th of May and the bear had not been out of hibernation very long. The hide was really nice though.

Brian with Tim and Yukon

Betty told me one time that she would like to try running dogs. When I was working at Prudhoe Bay in 1975, I worked with a man who built dog sleds. He was well known by dog mushers and had a good reputation as a sled builder. He and I were talking one day, and I mentioned that my wife wanted to try running dogs. I asked him if he would build a sled for her and he said he would. He told me as soon as he got back home he would start on it, and would let me know when it was ready.

Sometime later he sent me a letter and I went to his home and got the sled. It was beautiful, and the price was very reasonable. Tim and Yukon would get a workout now! They were both large dogs and about the same weight, so they would work well together. We got harnesses, rope, and whatever else was needed to get Betty started. It was a challenge for a while, because neither of the dogs had ever done this before and neither had Betty. She did good, though, and soon had the situation under control.

They were both gentle dogs, so she didn't have too much of a problem getting them harnessed up. She had the snow hook buried in the snow, and when she got both dogs ready she got on the runners, lifted the snow hook, gave them her signal, and they would take off out of there like a streak of lightning. Those two big dogs could really run.

Betty only had one bad experience. I was out on the trapline and she was home alone. She decided to go out and check the mail, so she got Tim and Yukon harnessed up and ready to go. There was a hump in the trail right at the start and the trail made a sharp turn at the top. The dogs were really excited and anxious to get going, and when they took off out of there they were going at top speed. The sled hit the hump, whipped around and slammed Betty into a tree, and hurt her shoulder. The sled tipped over, and the dogs were dragging her and the sled down the trail. She managed to hang on for a ways hollering, "Whoa!" but the dogs kept going. It finally got to be too much for her, and she had to let go.

She was really concerned that they might get hit by a car or by one of the many big trucks that traveled the Alaska Highway, if they went all the way to the road. She discovered later, by their tracks, that they had gone all the way to the mailbox, and just turned around and came back home. That was a big relief for Betty, and even though she was hurting bad, she was able to get their harnesses off and get them tied up.

When I got home she was just sitting in the cabin. She said to me, "I think I have a problem," and then told me what had happened. I took her to the doctor in Delta. He wanted her to go to Fairbanks to be checked by an orthopedic doctor. It was too late to go all the way to Fairbanks by then, and she sure didn't feel like being jostled around in our truck any more than she had to, so we got a room for her in a motel in Delta.

I came home and fed the dogs and got some supper and went to bed. The next morning I took her on into Fairbanks. The x-ray showed that she had a cracked shoulder blade. The doctor told us that there wasn't really anything that he could do; we would have to let it heal itself. She was pretty miserable for a while, but it healed up ok and she's still going strong!

We had gotten some more dogs, one of them being a female, so in a few years we had some puppies. Betty tried running a team of puppies and that was hilarious! They were a couple years old, so were big enough and strong enough to run. She thought it was difficult getting two dogs harnessed and ready to run, but when she tried those six puppies, she really had her hands full. They were jumping up and down, crawling all over each other, and getting their harnesses all tangled up. It was all that both of us could do to keep them lined out until she was ready to go.

Once they were ready, though, they would really run. She had to bury the snow hook in the snow, and also she had to tie the sled to a tree to keep them from taking off before she was ready. She really enjoyed it though, and ran dogs for about ten years. She even gave rides to friends occasionally.

Well, the dogs got old, and we got a road into our cabin, so we really didn't need them for getting the mail anymore. Betty said too, after that incident she was a little afraid of the sled, and it also got to be more work for her than fun so she gave it up. I tried it a couple times, but it didn't work out for me. My big boots stuck out sideways and kept hitting things and knocking my foot off the runners so I didn't bother with it. It really is fun though, and quiet! All you can hear is the rhythm of the dogs' feet on the trail, and the "ssshhhh" of the runners on the snow. You can also see more wildlife on a dog sled than you can on those noisy snow machines!

When you hear people say it's cruel to run dogs, don't you believe it! Those dogs love to run, and while you're getting them harnessed up, they are jumping up and down, whining, barking, squealing, and making every other kind of noise you can imagine until you're ready to go. Watch some dog races sometime and you'll see what I mean. Those mushers use a lot of dogs, and have to have several handlers to help them get their dogs harnessed and lined out.

47 A Close Call

Betty was home alone one day and decided she would go over to upper Dry Creek to visit some friends. I had cautioned her before to take her rifle with her if she went very far from the cabin. She also had a pistol, and this day she decided to carry that because the rifle gets heavy on a long hike. She is a short woman, and that long rifle was always catching in the brush and making walking difficult.

We had a trail between our cabin and the neighbors at the farm that followed an old moose trail. The woods and brush were quite thick in places, but there were some fairly open areas too. She was coming home in the late afternoon. As she walked along she said that several times she thought she caught a glimpse of something moving off to her right, but every time she looked, all she saw were big brown piles of spruce cones that the squirrels had piled up during the winter. There was a strong wind blowing, so it was difficult to hear anything above the rustling of leaves.

Well, bears don't make any noise while walking through the woods, but the wind would also help cover up any noise that Betty would have been making. She said that she was getting a little nervous thinking that there might be a bear nearby. She also was wishing she had brought her rifle with her. She had to watch the trail so she wouldn't trip over something, as well as keep a sharp eye out all around.

At one point, she looked ahead down the trail and froze in her tracks. There was a very large grizzly standing on the trail. She thought he was about 25 or 30 yards away. He was really close, and he was just as surprised as she was I guess, because he just stood there looking at her. She pulled out her little pistol, and asked God for help. The brush was at least three feet high, and the bear — on all four feet — stood well above it.

They stood there looking at each other for what seemed like a long time, but actually was probably only a few seconds. The bear didn't want any more of her than she did of him, and he suddenly turned and hightailed it back toward the plateau. What a relief! Betty thanked God for His protection, and got back to the cabin safely.

I might mention here that I'm not afraid of bears, but I have a very healthy respect for them. They are powerful beasts, and not to be taken lightly. They are also unpredictable. That bear could have just as well charged Betty, and that would have been the end of her. Even if she had had her rifle, at that close range, she probably would not have had a chance to use it. A bear could travel that distance in just a few seconds.

When we had our land surveyed, a surveyor came down from Fairbanks with his son for a helper. They surveyed the plots on the main branch of Dry Creek first, and then came over here to our place. They wanted to tie our survey in with Upper Dry Creek, and to do that he would have to go up on the plateau a ways so he could see both areas at the same time. He was using an instrument that required good light.

They got here in the late evening and he said that he would have to spend the night and do the work the next morning. He asked if his son could spend the night with us, because he planned to go up the side of the plateau a ways that evening. That way he could be situated and ready to go to work first thing in the morning. Of course, that was fine with us. He told his son to be ready at 4:00 a.m.

I asked him if he had a rifle and he said no, that he didn't need one. I guess he had surveyed in a lot of wilderness places and had never had any problems. I told him there were a lot of bears around here, and I offered to loan him a rifle. He said he wouldn't need it. I offered to take my rifle and go with him, but he said it wouldn't be necessary. He went up the side of the plateau a thousand feet or so, found a place by a large rock and went to sleep. It all turned out well. He got some sleep and didn't see any bears. In my opinion, though, he was very fortunate. It was a very careless and reckless thing to do, but he got away with it.

48 A Grizzly and Her Cubs

One summer in July, Brian and I spent eight days up on the plateau just looking the country over. We traveled light. We had a piece of plastic that we set up to sleep under, and took some dehydrated meals that just needed to be mixed with hot water. It was a great trip. The weather was warm and sunny.

One night we set up our lean-to just over on the lee side of Berry Creek Ridge so we would be out of the wind. Early the next morning I was happily sleeping away when Brian nudged me and said there was a bear nearby. I rose up and looked, and there was a grizzly, according to my rangefinder, about 600 yards away. It was trying to dig some varmint out of its hole, and was rolling rocks as big as bushel baskets down that slope. Brian said he thought the bear had cubs.

We watched, and sure enough there were two young cubs with her. She herself was light colored between her front and rear legs. Her legs, neck, and head were dark brown. She had one cub that was colored just like her, and the other one was all dark brown. They were playing around, jumping on each other and having great fun. They reminded me of a couple of young puppies when they play. I don't know if she got the varmint she was trying to dig out, but ten or fifteen minutes later she quit digging and headed our way. Berry Creek was down below us about 75 yards. The bears kept coming, and I was debating with myself about what to do if they got too close. A sow grizzly with cubs is a dangerous animal.

They kept coming, and it looked like they were headed for the creek below us, and would not be coming up where we were so we just stayed still and waited. What an impressive bear—she was the largest bear I've seen so far in the wild. They went into the brush below us and disappeared.

We had one thing going for us—convection currents. In the morning when the air is warming, the air flows upward. This morning the air was coming from them to us, so they would not get our scent. Nevertheless, I told Brian that if they came back out of the brush and headed up our way, we would have to stand up and let her know we were there. Actually, at 75 yards they were already too close, but there we were and we'd have to make the best of it. I did not want to have to shoot her.

In a few minutes they came back out of the brush and headed right back where they came from, and disappeared into the brush. Very good! I still was amazed at her size. I have no doubt that I could have dispatched her if she had charged us, but I was sure glad she didn't. They never knew we were there. I sat there with my big .300 Winchester magnum rifle, and it seemed like it was a BB gun to me as I watched that big bear walking away. I guess I could say that was the highlight of our trip, even though we saw another grizzly and a very large bull moose.

We were gradually working our way back to our cabin and stopped to rest. The area was abundant with small ponds and ridges running all around. As I sat there looking around, I saw a dark grizzly about a hundred yards away. He was loping along towards the area we had just come from. I told Brian which way to look and he would see a bear. Just a few seconds later the bear broke out of the brush, went out into one of the ponds and sat down. It was a hot day and he needed to cool off. He sat there about ten minutes, came out of the pond, shook himself off, and continued on his journey. I don't know where he was headed, but the last time we saw him, he was two miles away and still running.

We sat there for a while longer. The next thing I saw was a big bull moose. He crossed a narrow place in the trees and disappeared. I told Brian about it and said that when we left there we would try to see him again. We walked slowly and carefully and moved as quietly as possible. We hadn't seen him, and we came to a low ridge about eight feet high. I thought he might be on the other side so we crawled up the side of the ridge on our hands and knees.

Sure enough, there he was. He was lying down in the grass near a small pond. He was only 25 yards away so we got a good look at him. He, too, was an impressive animal. I guessed that he had a 60"or 65" rack; when he turned his head, his antlers reached past his rump. While we were watching he got up and turned towards us. He looked like he was three feet wide across his chest. Probably wasn't, but he was big. When hunting season came around I was going to come back and try to get him. We backed off quietly, and came on home.

The following September, a friend from Wisconsin was here visiting. He was a hunter, and when I told him about that big bull he was ready to go. He, Brian, and I got our stuff together and headed up the East Fork. We set up camp on a ridge overlooking a large pond. It was too late to do any hunting, so we built a fire and had some supper.

While we were eating, a pack of wolves not too far away started howling. That was really nice to hear. There were high voices, medium voices, and one very deep voice. They were hunting and working their way around ponds and ridges. It was starting to get dark so we finished our supper and went to bed. We could still hear them off in the distance.

Brian moose hunting on the Plateau

If I remember correctly, we hunted for four days. The only moose we saw was an old cow. We were a little disappointed, but I guess it was for the best that we didn't get a moose there. It was five miles from the cabin, and we would have had to make several trips to pack it all out. We would have had to walk in the creek all the way, and it would have been a tough pack.

49 Boring Holes in the Sky

When I was a boy I was very interested in airplanes. Like a lot of boys and some girls my age, I used to buy those kits for model airplanes. You had to cut the parts out of balsa wood with a razor blade, glue them together on a pattern, and cover it all with a special paper. Then you'd sprinkle the paper with water and it would tighten up on the frame. They were small, maybe a 24" wingspan, and powered with a rubber band. They would fly too. We would turn the propeller to wind the rubber band (in those days, they were real rubber), hold the prop with one hand, and hold the plane in the other. Then we would push the plane and let go of the prop at the same time. A good flight was probably 25 or 30 feet.

When I had to go to Anchorage for prosthetic work, we usually stayed at the Big Timber Motel on 5th Avenue. It was right next to Merrill Field. I had quite a lot of time after seeing my prosthetist, and I would sit out by the fence and watch the airplanes take off and land. It wasn't long until that old love for airplanes got a hold of me and I decided I needed an airplane.

It would be very useful for me because I could fly around and spot game, land, and go get it. Not the same day, of course, because that was illegal, but at least I'd know where they probably would be the next day. I could think of all kinds of benefits an airplane would provide. Betty was kind of quiet, but she didn't say "no." I did get a modest settlement from my accident, so I had enough money to buy an airplane. I bought an older Super Cub. They are the airplanes for Alaska. It was a 1960 model, with a 150 horsepower engine. I bought it in Fairbanks, found a flight instructor who flew it to Delta for me, and I began taking flying lessons.

This was great! I sure loved flying. I flew my first solo flight on November 13, 1984, and got my private pilot's license on August 8, 1985. I bought some Landis snow skis for it too. It had large tundra tires for landing on places other than airports, and I had a belly tank installed for extra fuel. It also had an extended baggage compartment, which would prove to be a real asset. I was very happy with the whole set up. Betty enjoyed flying with me, and we shared a lot of happy hours up there "boring holes in the sky."

In February of 1983, I had my plane in the hangar in Delta getting some work done on it. One day a guy came in and started up a conversation. His name was Bob also, and he had just moved from Montana to the Delta Junction area. He was also a pilot, and he had a Super Cub. He was one of those people who made you feel like you'd known him all your life. We got to be good friends, and did a lot of flying together. His wife liked to fly also.

He had a friend who owned a hunting and fishing lodge on the Unalakleet River, just upstream from the village of Unalakleet, which is in western Alaska on the shore of Norton Sound. The river was eating the bank away near his buildings, and he was afraid that the bank would finally give way and he would lose his lodge. Bob had a friend just south of Fairbanks who was an engineer, and the lodge owner wanted him to go over and see if there was anything that could be done to save his place.

Bob was going to fly him over, and asked me if I wanted to fly along with them. He didn't have to ask twice. That sounded like an adventure and I was ready go. The engineer's name was Brad. He flew with Bob, and I followed along in my plane. We had to carry extra gas with us, and we landed on the Yukon River near Ruby to re-fuel. We usually had hot coffee or hot chocolate so we would take a break and have a cup.

Kaltag is a small village on the Yukon River just downstream from Galena. When we flew over Kaltag I decided that when we came back I would get a picture of it. It was a small village nestled in between the mountains and the river and even had an airstrip. We spent several days in Unalakleet while Brad looked the situation over. I played some chess with the caretaker for a little relaxation. I don't remember what suggestions Brad made about the river, but the time came for us to head for home. We had refueled our planes so we filled our extra cans and took off.

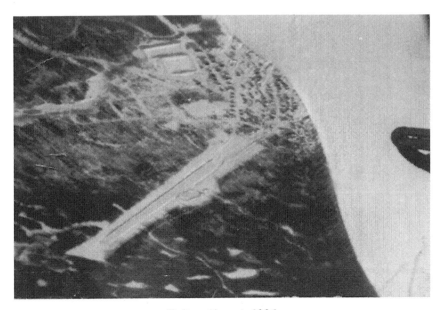

Kaltag Airport, 1986

We had already flown past Kaltag, when I remembered that I wanted to get a picture. I called Bob on the radio and told him I was going to circle back and get the picture and I would catch up with him. He said ok so I turned back, got my picture, and got back on course for home. It was a beautiful day. I was in a euphoric state of mind, really enjoying the trip, when Bob's voice came in over the radio. He said, "Hey, Bob, we've got to do something different!" I said, "What do you mean?" He said, "Look behind you."

We had been flying for at least ten minutes since I took the picture. I looked back and I could still see Kaltag. We had one heck of a head wind! Bob asked me to radio Galena, and find out what the surface wind velocity was. He was going to drop down as low as he could to see if we could get out of the wind.

The Yukon River makes a big bend upstream from Galena, and the course we were on would take us back to the river and we could drop down farther and get below the trees on the bank. I found out that the surface winds at Galena were around 6 knots. Not bad at all, so maybe Bob's plan would work. We got to the river and dropped down to about ten feet above the riverbed and we were out of the wind.

Yukon River, March 1986

Bob is a much more experienced pilot than I. If I had been flying alone that day, in my euphoric state of mind, I might have just kept churning along through the sky until I ran out of gas. On the other hand, I think that if I had been alone I would have been more attentive to my environment rather than depending on Bob so much. I learned a very valuable lesson that day.

Another time Bob called me and told me he was going to fly out to the Wood River Lodge, and did I want to fly along. He knew the owners and wanted to visit them. I certainly did so Betty and I hopped in the Cub and met him in Delta. Cubs are only two-place planes so Bob had to fly alone in his Cub. The lodge was a very nice place. We spent an hour or so there and took off for home.

On the way back we flew right past Mt. Hayes. Mt. Hayes looks like a head and shoulders. It has a high peak in the center with two flat places on each side. It is a great landmark; you can see it for many miles. We flew up and flew a 360-degree circle around the high peak. Almost every time I see that mountain now, I remember that flight. It was fun!

On the Unalakleet River, March 1986

50 Friends Helping Friends

One time Paul was flying with me. In Alaska it is legal to land on a road as long as you don't interfere with vehicle traffic. We were flying from Dry Creek to Dot Lake. I could land on the highway right by his house and drop him off, sort of like a taxicab service.

He had a favorite hunting camp nearby so I decided to fly over it; maybe we could see a moose. This was a couple of months before moose season, but Alaskans are always on the lookout for a possible place to get some fresh meat. In an open place, just below his camp, was a very large bull moose. That was exciting, especially for Paul, and he was hoping that bull would still be in the area come September 1st.

Our neighbors at the farm had acquired some property up on the plateau near Fish Lake. They were in the process of moving building materials up there. They built a log cabin from the trees right there, but they needed 2x4's, windows, boards for the floor and lumber for door and window frames.

This is where the extended baggage compartment came in handy. I could get eight foot 2 x 4's and boards in there, and I tied the windows to the lift struts. I made several trips and hauled a lot of the stuff they needed. They also hauled stuff up by snow machine and sled from Dot Lake.

I had snow skis on my plane and it was a cloudy day. When the sun is shining, snow ski flying is great because you can see where the snowdrifts are and avoid them when landing. On one of my landings on this cloudy day, I hit a drift, and broke a hydraulic unit, which was like a shock absorber on the landing gear. I had safety cables on the gear, so they held the plane up and prevented the propeller from striking anything. But what to do now?

Fish Lake Landing, 1986

I turned my radio on and transmitted my numbers, to see if any other pilots were in the area. I could hardly believe my ears. Bob and his wife were up flying around, heard me, and answered. I told him where I was and what had happened, and he radioed back that they would come right over. He flew to Delta, got a new hydraulic unit, helped me get it installed, and went on his way. That was easy. Good friends. I taxied over, unloaded my cargo and flew back to Dry Creek.

In 1994, I built a 24 by 32 foot two-story garage. We had a lot of large spruce trees on our property. A friend of mine had a band-saw mill that he let me use, and Dick let me use his bucket loader to move the logs around and lift them up on the saw table. One of Karl's sons, Toby, came over and helped me, and we sawed all the framing lumber and boards to build the first story of the garage. We also had enough boards for the floor of the second story.

I bought lumber from my neighbors at Dry Creek Logging and Milling, and Ron and Jason and some others helped me get the upstairs framed in, the trusses up and even helped get the metal roof on. Paul and several other men from the farm helped on that job too. Ron made a large wood burning stove for us out of a piece of oil pipeline pipe. It is heavy, but it sure works well. It is made of 24" diameter pipe and 30" long. I sure have appreciated that garage and stove. In the winter, it's usually 15 to 20 degrees warmer in the garage than it is outside, even without any fire in the stove.

Our garage with Wild Fireweed in in foreground

After the garage was built I moved my workshop from the converted hay barn to the garage. One day, Betty and I were sitting around drinking coffee and talking. The subject of the now empty hay barn came up and what we might use it for. Suddenly, her face lit up and she said "how about a guest cabin?" Good idea!

Occasionally, family or friends would come to visit, and if we had a place for them to stay overnight, it would be really nice. When I first closed the building in for a workshop, I insulated it with 4-inch fiberglass insulation, so now I went to Delta and got some OSB plywood for the walls and ceiling.

Betty wanted to call it the "Blue Room" so we painted the walls three feet up a dark blue, and from there a light blue on up to and including the ceiling. Betty had a clothes rack next to the wood stove to dry her laundry on. One time while we were gone, the rack tipped over onto the stove and a lot of her clothes burned up and the place was full of black soot! We were fortunate that it didn't burn down, but now it was a real mess! We cleaned it up, and I painted the floor brown and the walls and ceiling a straw color and we called it "The Haybarn." After all, that's what it was originally!

It served us well for a lot of years, but finally it started looking a little dingy, so Eileen, Pam and two of our great-granddaughters came down and painted the whole inside some very nice light pastel colors, and bought new curtains for the windows and door. It really looks nice—in my opinion, it's better than the Hilton. It is a very pleasant place to spend a night, or more!

51 Adventures in the Clear Blue Sky

The folks at the Dry Creek Community, or "the farm" as the rest of us called it, referred to themselves as "the Land." They were of a certain religious persuasion, and came from all over the lower 48, and some came from other countries. All of us who live in the area are part of the community, of course, but those terms served to differentiate between them and the other local residents.

In the early years, the mid-1970's, they had somewhere around 200 people living there. They worked the land with horses, planted hay and oat crops to feed the horses and cows, and raised pigs and chickens. They had a large vegetable garden every year and one of their main crops was potatoes. They shared their bounty with their neighbors too. They also had a logging and milling operation, and they used the horses for that too. That was 40 years ago. Now they have modern equipment for it all, but they still use their horses for farming along with the machinery. They also have their own K-12 school.

One year I offered to take any high school graduates who were interested for an airplane ride. One of the young ladies wanted to go. She had never been to their cabin up at the lake, so I told her I would fly her up there so she could see it from the air, and also see the lay of the land. A Super Cub is the way to see Alaska!

There was a high ridge I had to fly over, and just before we got to it, I looked down and saw three grizzly bears about halfway up the side of the ridge. It was a sow with two cubs. The sow was light blonde color with dark brown head and legs. She had one cub colored like her, and the other was all dark brown. I was reminded of the bears that Brian and I had seen a few years before. It could have been the same sow. We were only a few miles from the area where he and I had seen them.

My passenger couldn't see them from the back seat so I did a slow, shallow turn. When we came back around, the sow stood up on her hind legs swinging her front legs like she was swatting flies and the cubs ran up the hill as fast as they could go. We were only about 200 feet above them. I circled several times, and each time we came back they did the same thing. I was really enjoying it and thought my passenger was too.

Then I remembered that this was her first airplane ride. "How ya doin' back there?" I asked. She answered in a low, sort of weak voice, "ok," but I knew from the sound of her voice that she was probably having some air sickness, so I leveled the plane and headed on toward the cabin. I always enjoy seeing wildlife. Whenever I had someone in my airplane, I was always careful and considerate of them. I know pilots who are not considerate, and they think it's great fun if they can make someone sick. They are few and far between, but they are out there. I always tried to make my passenger's flight a fun experience.

I also took one of the young men up for a ride. We flew over their cabin. He had been there before, but had never seen it from the air. We flew around just looking at the scenery. We flew up higher in the mountains, and saw a flock of fifteen or twenty Dall sheep. They are beautiful white animals, and the eastern Alaska Range is claimed to be the best Dall sheep hunting in the world. The meat is excellent. I've never hunted sheep because it takes some rugged climbing to get up to where they live, and I just couldn't make it. I don't remember if my passenger got one that year, but he did eventually go up and get one.

One time Ed and T.J. stopped by on their way to go caribou hunting up in the Fortymile country. They were going to drive up the Taylor Highway to the village of Eagle, on the bank of the Yukon River. There they would hire a pilot to fly them approximately 30 miles west to Alder Creek, where there is an airstrip on top of a hill. They mentioned that if I had the time, maybe I'd like to fly my plane up there and hunt with them. That sounded good to me, so a couple of days later I loaded my hunting gear in the Super Cub and flew up there.

When I was learning to fly I had to do some long cross-country flying. As well as using my charts to navigate, I also learned how to recognize the terrain below by looking at a chart of the country and spotting the actual landmarks below as I was flying over them. A river, a creek, a valley, or a mountain peak confirmed that I was where I was supposed to be. It is very reassuring to be able to do that. At first it was difficult, but I soon caught on to it and it was fun. It's quite easy when you're flying over civilization with farms, cities, or lots of roads, but it's a whole lot different when there is nothing below you but nature. I practiced that on the way to Alder Creek.

It's difficult to get lost while flying in Alaska. When I was learning to fly my instructor told me that if I ever did get lost, to just climb higher. There are many mountains, and you can see them for hundreds of miles and you can know exactly where you are. I found Alder Creek ok, landed and set up camp. We built a fire, had some supper, and went to sleep. It was a short distance from the airstrip to the ridge where they were hunting. I found a good place where I could see, and sat down to watch, hoping that a caribou would show up.

I didn't see any caribou that day, but I did see a grizzly. He was on the next ridge to the east of the one I was on, with a deep gorge between us. I would estimate that he was three hundred yards away. I spotted him walking along the ridge to the south. Suddenly, he stood up on his hind legs. He had his nose high like he smelled something, and then he turned and hightailed it back the way he had come. I have no idea what was out there but whatever it was, that bear wanted no part of it.

If I remember correctly, I hunted two more days. Ed and T.J. had gotten a caribou and had laid their signal flag out indicating that they were ready to go, if their pilot should fly over checking on them. I loaded my gear in the plane, and was getting ready to take off, when Ed said, "Hey, there's a caribou!" I looked down the runway a couple hundred yards and there was a caribou walking across.

I got my rifle out of the plane and loaded it. By that time the caribou had disappeared in the brush. I walked down there anyway, thinking he might show up again, or maybe I'd see another one. I was looking in the direction the caribou had gone, when I caught a glimpse of movement out of the corner of my eye, to the left. There came another bull caribou so I shot him. It doesn't get any better than this. I taxied my plane right up to him, processed him and loaded him in the plane. No backpacking on this trip! I flew home, a very happy hunter with some fresh meat.

52 Panning for Gold

We owned some gold mining property on a creek up on the Steese Highway, near Central, Alaska. We didn't get up there very often, because it was about 250 miles each way. We talked about going up there on the 4th of July weekend one year, and our grandson T.J. wanted to go with us. We still had our little travel trailer, so we loaded our stuff in and took off up there. We drove down to the creek and unhitched the trailer.

I had a Ford Aerostar at the time, and it was all wheel drive. It was six miles up the creek to our property. The trail wound around in the creek bed and the local miners were supposed to keep it open, but they had gotten a little careless, and right at the beginning of the trail there was a very steep place which also had quite a steep slope sideways to it as well. Well, no problem, right? I had 4-wheel drive, so no problem!

We piled in the Aerostar and took off. It seems that I *might* have *slightly* misjudged how steep it was, and also how much it tilted sideways! What a ride! For a few minutes we were really sweating it! I don't really know how we kept the car from rolling down that bank, but T.J. and Betty were both out there pushing and I'm sure that was one reason we didn't!

We made it on up to the good part of the trail without wrecking our car, and got on up to the property with no other problems. Of course, we had our gold pans and a shovel with us, so we started to pan out some of the gravel. In my very first pan, I got a nugget about an eighth of an inch in diameter. Hey guys, look, I'm rich!!! That was the last nugget though; from then on we just got small flakes of gold. There was some bedrock sticking up out of the creek bed, and it was cracked up badly. I took the little trowel I had with me, and scraped some sand out of the cracks and panned it out. There were a lot of really tiny flakes of gold in it.

We visited the gold room at the University of Alaska in Fairbanks one time. There was a wonderful display of gold nuggets. There were very large ones, and they decreased in size right down to what is called "dust" it is so fine. A sign said that an ounce of gold was equivalent to a level teaspoon full of the gold dust. I don't know how long it would have taken to get a teaspoon full of the dust we were finding, but I think we would starve to death trying to make a living at it.

It was really exciting and we had a lot of fun. To get any amount of gold out of there, however, a person would need some machinery: a small bulldozer, or a front-end loader, and a sluice box. We could have built a sluice box, but we couldn't afford to buy any machinery, so we eventually sold the property. We never heard if the buyer ever did anything with it or not.

I'd like to explain a little about panning gold. It is actually very easy; you just need to know a few basics. After you get some gravel in your pan, you put it in the water and move it in small circles to agitate the gravel. You pick out the larger stones and roots, taking care to wash all of the dirt off into the pan. You just keep moving the pan in circles while tipping it forward to allow the gravel to wash over the front edge of the pan. You can take the pan out of the water and continue the same way. When the water is all gone, just dip it back in the creek, or washtub, if you are practicing in your backyard, and continue until all you have is very fine stuff in the pan.

Gold is very heavy and if you are careful, and just let the gravel wash over the edge of the pan slowly you will not lose any gold. You might have some black sand in your pan, which is called magnetite. It is very heavy too, but not as heavy as gold. It is said that where there is gold, there will also be black sand, but not necessarily the other way around. You can have black sand, but no gold. I have done a lot of panning in the East Fork, and have gotten a lot of black sand, but there is no gold in it.

One way you can practice panning gold is to put some lead bird shot in the pan with the gravel. Any size shot will work. I suggest at least a half dozen pieces. Pan it out like I explained, and see how many shot are left in the pan when you are finished. If there is the same number left that you started with, you have done a great job, and you can certainly pan gold. Gold is more than three times heavier than lead, so if you can save all of the lead pellets, you can surely save the gold. You can practice panning anywhere, and if you ever get to a place where there is gold you will be ready to have some fun! Why, you might even find something valuable right there in your own backyard!

53 Travelling "Outside"

"Outside" is what Alaskans call any place outside of Alaska. I guess I was feeling adventurous. I had been thinking of flying my plane back to Michigan to see my son Rob and his family. Bob told me one day that he was going to fly out to Montana to see his dad and brother. He wondered if I would like to fly out with him. Yes, I surely would! I could fly to Montana, spend a day or two, and then fly on to Michigan. It was ok with Betty, so I got ready to go.

It was an exciting time for me—landing at a different airport every day, and seeing all of that country from the air. When we landed somewhere to spend the night, we just rolled our sleeping bags out under the wing, and had a good night's sleep. I did spend a couple of days in Montana and enjoyed it. On the way to Michigan I stopped in Wisconsin to see our friend Dennis and his wife, and some other friends there. I got to Gaylord, Michigan just fine. Ed's folks had told me I could stay with them while I was there and they were at the airport to pick me up. I spent about a month there, and stayed busy taking the family for airplane rides and visiting.

The only problem I'd had so far, was when I was flying over the Upper Peninsula of Michigan. One of the magnetos quit working, and the engine was running really rough. Fortunately, I was only about ten miles from an airport so I was able to land safely and get it repaired. It happened to be the town where some old friends of mine lived, so they gave me a bed for the night, and the next day I was on my way. When I left Michigan, I flew back to Wisconsin and spent a couple of more days with Dennis.

I had a friend in Wyoming and decided to fly around that way to see him. I had been in touch with Bob, and we were going to meet up somewhere along the way and fly back to Alaska together. When I left Wisconsin, I flew generally southwest to Nebraska, then flew toward the southeast corner of Wyoming. I had been flying for about twelve hours. At one point in western Nebraska I flew over a little airstrip and thought, "I should just land there and spend the night." It looked like a quiet little place. All day I had heard weather reports of high winds ahead, and possibly some thunderstorms. Maybe I was so tired that I wasn't thinking straight, but I kept on going.

I was looking below for landmarks, and nothing was looking right. I flew over a four-lane highway I didn't recognize, so I decided to go down and see what it was. It was Interstate 25, and I saw a sign pointing west to Ft. Collins, Colorado. Once again the wind had pulled a fast one on me, and I was way south of where I wanted to be. I decided to land at Ft. Collins. Well, the wind wasn't through with me yet! From the time I flew downwind, turned to the base leg, and turned to the final leg for landing, the wind had turned almost 180 degrees, and was coming from my right rear quarter.

If I had been a more experienced pilot, I would probably have aborted the landing, but I proceeded to land. The wind was very strong behind me, and I couldn't keep the plane tracking down the runway, resulting in a ground loop. I got it off the runway ok, and got permission to tie it down at a hangar nearby. I spent some time in Ft. Collins getting the plane repaired. One of the mechanics let me use a room in his basement; it was a very comfortable place. He felt sorry for me because I had set my tent up on the tarmac, and had just got it ready when the wind got a hold of it, and it went tumbling down the taxiway. The area was all blacktop, and I had no way to stake it down.

When the plane was ready, I took off for Wyoming. I took my friend for a ride, spent the night with him and left the next day. I had called Bob and told him what had happened, and he said he needed to get home, so he would go on ahead. I plotted my course to the next airport where I would fuel the plane up. Surprise, surprise! When I got there, the runway was painted with an "X." They had just laid new blacktop and the airport was closed.

Well, I had to land. I had planned my fuel consumption to that airport. Fortunately for me, that work had been done a couple of days before—as I found out after I landed—so my big tundra tires never even marked the runway. A guy came over and at first was a little upset because I had landed. I explained my situation and that I didn't have enough fuel to get to the next airport. While planning my flight I should have checked on the conditions at that airport. My mistake.

He told me that the airport was closed, and there was no fuel available, but there was a gas station across the road where I could fuel up. I taxied my Cub out the gate, across the road and right up to the gas pump, and filled my tanks. You may wonder if that was legal. Yes, I had a Supplemental Type Certificate (STC), for using automotive gas in my engine. The guy told me it would be ok to take off on the runway, so I was on my way again.

The only other problem I had coming back was at Whitehorse, Yukon Territory. I had taken off from Watson Lake with no problems. Upon landing at Whitehorse, I had difficulty steering my plane. The tail wheel is connected to the rudder pedals so you can steer the plane while on the ground. Something was very wrong! I managed to get off the runway, and got out to see what the problem was.

The tail wheel was flat. What caused the tire to go flat while flying through the air I'll never know. I suppose it was possible to have picked up a nail or something on my take off run. I don't recall now what the reason was. The mechanic put a new tube in it, and I continued on to the gas pump, filled my tanks and took off for home.

Northway, Alaska, is the Customs Office for planes flying up the Alaska Highway so I landed and took care of that. I landed at Dry Creek, tied the plane down, filled the gas tanks, and my trip was over. It was a fun trip, a good experience, and as almost every time I flew, I learned a few things.

We also made a couple of trips Outside in our truck. On one trip we took Pam out to Iowa to go to college. On the same trip we took Brian to spend some time with his biological father. He spent a couple of years there while attending high school. When Pam graduated, we went and got them both and came the long way home. We wanted to see the Grand Tetons in Wyoming, so we went around that way

Wouldn't you know it? When we went through the area it was foggy and rainy, and we couldn't even see them. We did go through Yellowstone Park though, and that was very interesting. We saw the "Old Faithful" geyser too!

54 Last Hunt on Macomb Plateau

Another hunting story! The year after Festus died, one of my neighbors, Mark, told me he was going up caribou hunting, and asked me if I wanted to go. I had never even considered that, considering the fact that I would have to walk, but I really do like to hunt up on the plateau. It was a long trail though, and I wasn't sure my leg could handle it. Well, it did seem like an adventure, so I decided to give it a try. It's difficult to get everything you need for a hunting trip into a pack that weighs less than 45 or 50 pounds.

I hiked over to Mark's place, and we took off. We had approximately three days' worth of food with us, and if we were lucky, that would be enough. We spent the first night about two-thirds of the way up the side of the plateau. That was all that my leg could take for one day. The next morning we got a pretty good start, but even so, it was six o'clock that evening by the time we got to my caribou camp.

My leg was pretty sore, but we made it, and I could take it easy now. That is, until we got a caribou, then I would have to be on my feet some more. The weather was nice, clear skies and sunshine. Too nice, I guess, because we were there three days, and hadn't seen any caribou. We got up the fourth day and Mark told me that he was going back down to get some more food.

He came back up the next day, and I told him that I had spotted a small bunch of caribou just before dark the day he left. They were about a mile away, and even though we couldn't see them now, I thought they would be somewhere nearby. The terrain was quite rolling, and they could appear and disappear at a moment's notice.

We took off to see if we could find them. Sure enough, we got to where we could see around one high place, and spotted a half dozen caribou lying down, and one of them was a nice bull. Mark said for me to take him and he would go on up Berry Creek Ridge and try to find another one, so I shot the bull. There was a large boulder near the top of Berry Creek Ridge, where one could almost always find caribou if one was willing to sit and wait.

I suggested to Mark that it might be a good place to check out. I mentioned that about a hundred yards beyond that boulder would be a good place to watch. He took off, and I went to work on my caribou. Bending over for long periods of time skinning an animal was hard on my back, so I stood up often and stretched out. One time, I looked up towards Berry Creek Ridge, and saw a herd of probably 25 or 30 caribou. They were on the downhill side of the boulder, so I didn't know if Mark had seen them.

They were running hard, so I suspected that something had spooked them, but I hadn't heard any rifle shots. I was afraid they had seen Mark, but he hadn't seen them.

I was saying in my mind, "Mark, look down the hill!" There were a couple of very nice bulls in the herd too. I kept thinking, "Mark, look down the hill!" My heart sank to think that he wouldn't get one of them, but then I heard a shot! All right, he had seen them and got a nice bull.

It took the rest of the day to get them processed and back to camp. Mark had to pack his two miles, and mine was almost a mile from camp. We were sure ready for some supper that night. There was no way that we could pack them out on our backs—at least I couldn't. Mark could get his out in two trips, but it was almost impossible for me. My leg had raw spots on it and was really sore. It would have been a tough trip for me to just walk back, not to mention packing meat.

The next morning Mark told me that he was going down to get some horses to pack the meat out. Well, that was music to my ears! I spent the day pretty close to camp. I saw a black wolf that afternoon, but no other animals. I was still thinking of that long trail back, and wondering how long it would take me to get home. Morning came and Mark showed up with three horses, two to pack the meat, and one for me to ride. Another neighbor came along to lead the other horse. I sure did appreciate them being so considerate of me. That was a fun time, good friends, a good hunt, and good caribou meat.

Mark and crew with horses to the rescue

However, that was my last hunt on Macomb Plateau. I have no regrets though. Old Festus and I had many good hunts up there, and I have lots of good memories. I appreciated that Mark talked me into going up there with him, because I really did enjoy it all. I sure do love that high country!

55 Ms. Anne

We had a friend named Anne, who had come to Alaska to teach school in Chicken, Alaska. She arrived in Eagle, Alaska on the Yukon River. There was a transporter in Eagle with packhorses who would take her and some other folks to Chicken.

They were riding along the trail and one of the other women on the trip noticed that one of the man's socks kept slipping down. Several times she told him, "Hey mister, one of your socks is slipping down." After a few times of that, he reigned in his horse, reached in his saddle bag, got out a hammer and a nail, pulled his sock up, and nailed it to his leg! He put the hammer back in the saddlebag, tipped his hat to the woman and rode on. Anne said the woman almost fell off her horse. She didn't know the guy had a wooden leg! You can read more about Anne's adventures in the book "Tisha" by Robert Specht.

Anne had gotten sick and was staying with her friend Jackie in Dot Lake because she was not able to stay alone. Well, Anne's condition grew worse, and she passed away there in the month of April.

I don't remember the year, but I think it was in the late 80's. Paul was the pastor of Dot Lake Chapel. His wife, Martha, and Linda, a friend from the children's home, would prepare the body for burial. Both of the women were nurses, so they knew what to do, and Paul built a casket for her.

In Alaska, a deceased body does not have to be embalmed, but is supposed to be buried within 24 hours. Anne's husband Fred and two of their foster children were buried at their home place in Chicken, and Anne wanted to be buried there also. We didn't know if anyone was digging the grave, or if anyone in Chicken even knew of her passing.

I decided to fly to Chicken and flew over her house to see if a grave was being dug. There was no sign at all of anyone around, so I landed at the airstrip and walked the mile or so up to one of her neighbor's houses. No one in Chicken had heard of Anne's passing. I told him that her body was being prepared, and we were supposed to have her in the ground within 24 hours. I asked him if he could dig the grave. He looked at me for a minute and said, "Bob, this early in the spring, there could be six feet of frost in the ground up here." but he would see what he could do.

I flew back to Dot Lake, landed on the road and taxied over to a place where I could tie my plane down. I told them what I had found and what the man had told me. Paul called someone and explained our problem, and they told him to do the best he could and get her buried as soon as possible. They had everything ready to go. Paul and Martha, Jackie, Jackie's sister, Anne's foster daughter Lynn, and Betty and I all went to Chicken with Anne.

That was a long time ago, and I don't remember the neighbor's name, but he had gone over to the gravesite, built a fire on it, and laid some sheets of corrugated metal roofing over that to keep the heat in. Before we went to sleep that night, we put more wood on the fire and replaced the metal roofing. The neighbor came over the next morning with his backhoe. I think it was a sort of a miracle, because he was able to break through the frost and dig the grave. We had a graveside service for Anne and went back home.

I've been back there a couple of times since then. Anne's foster daughter, Lynn, used to go back and spend the summers there, but I don't know if she still does that or not. Later, Paul made a marker for Anne's grave. It's always sad to lose a dear friend, but it's also encouraging to know that there is someone who will take care of the details when one passes on. Anne knew she had that kind of friends. So there she lies, with her husband and daughters, waiting for that glorious Resurrection for those who are looking for Jesus Christ's return.

56 A Foggy Landing

In late summer one year, a friend asked me if I would fly him to a place where he could hunt sheep. I wasn't familiar with the place where he wanted to go, and I wasn't even sure I wanted to do it, but I decided to go and look the area over. A pilot who was familiar with the area, told me of a small landing strip near where I was going. I asked Karl if he would like to go with me to check it out. He certainly did. I called Bob, and told him where I was going, and that if I didn't fly over his house by seven o'clock that evening, I was in trouble. It's always a good idea to do that when flying to a remote area.

Just before we took off from Dry Creek, Karl's wife put two cans of sardines in his pocket. I didn't plan to be gone more than five or six hours, so I didn't take any food. It was about 70 miles as the crow flies to the area I wanted to look over, so that would take no more than an hour's flight, one way, depending on the wind.

We had a good flight. The weather was cloudy and cool, and the air was smooth. Karl got some nice pictures along the way. We found the little airstrip, and I circled it several times to check it out. It was quite short, around 300 feet, and it went slightly up hill from east to west. It looked good so I landed. We were a quarter mile or so west of the Trident Glacier. Karl said he'd like to get some pictures of the glacier and the surrounding area, so he took off down there. Karl is an excellent photographer and he got some nice pictures.

*Johnson Glacier ***

*Trident Glacier 1987 ***

Pre-flight check before taking off from Trident Glacier area *

There is a saying in Alaska that the mountains make their own weather, and that is very true. I checked the oil, looked around the engine compartment, did a walk around to check everything out, and prepared for take-off. I had also been watching the weather, and noticed that there was some fog forming along the tops of the hills. I walked down and told Karl we needed to get going. By the time we got back to the plane the fog had come down to about 400 feet, and there was a light rain falling.

Trident Glacier, August 1987 *

It would take more distance for my take off run because moist air is less dense than dry air, and the wings wouldn't get as much lift. No problem, we had plenty of room and got airborne just fine. The fog was moving in fast. We got down over the glacier, and the only opening there was in the fog was to the north, down the glacier. I banked the plane around, and headed for the opening. Before we got there, however, the opening had closed up.

I did a 180-degree turn, and headed back up the glacier. There was a high ridge to my left and I could still see the top so I started climbing. I got up over the ridge into a large valley. I circled the valley several times looking for a way out, but there wasn't one. On my last trip around, I got into the fog. I held the plane in a bank, and came back over the ridge into the valley. I knew then that I had to land somewhere!

The reason I hadn't landed sooner was because I didn't see any place down there where I thought I could land safely. There was a small creek, but the whole area was very uneven and strewn with large rocks, and there were large pools of water all over the place. I had no choice now. I firmly believed that I had to try to make a controlled landing, or I would be making an uncontrolled landing, which probably would not turn out well!

Suddenly, there was a really bright spot that had opened up to the south, and I thought it might be a way out. I headed for it, but something inside me was screaming, "No, No, don't do it, go back!" I turned back, and set the plane up for a slow flight. A Super Cub will fly around 40 miles an hour. I circled around slowly, and headed up the hill, and pretty much just let the plane land itself. We touched down, bounced once, and the plane stopped. The engine was still running, both the wings were still attached to the plane, and everything seemed to be ok. There is an old saying among pilots that any landing you can walk away from was a good landing! I made a good landing that day. I took a minute to thank the Lord for a safe landing.

I cut the engine and climbed out to check the plane. There was a small bend in the left lower longeron, just enough to wrinkle the fabric a little. The plane had hit the ground and bounced up over a two-foot bank, and just plopped down and stopped. The attach point for the right gear leg was broken, but again the safety cables held the plane up so the prop did not strike the ground. We were two very happy people.

We were thankful for a good landing *

Karl told me that during all of this he had been talking to the Lord, and he mentioned to Him that he wasn't ready to die yet, and that he still had a lot of things he wanted to do. He said the Lord must have heard him.

I got on the radio and tried to contact someone to let them know of our predicament. I couldn't raise anyone so I turned the radio off to save the battery. I would try again the next morning. Karl opened his cans of sardines. I don't care for them myself so he ate them all. I had a quart bottle of some special tablets for just such a time as this. A dozen or so of them, they said, was equal to a whole meal. I took one of the sardine cans, drained some gasoline from a wing tank, and heated some water for coffee. Well, I didn't have any coffee with me, but I heated the water and handed a cup to Karl. I said, "Karl, here's a cup of hot water. You can have coffee, tea, hot chocolate, whatever you want; you just have to use your imagination a little." He laughed, took a sip of hot water, and remarked, "Hmmm, not bad!" We both had a good laugh.

After the Landing *

The fog was still very thick. We walked around the area to see if there was a place where we could take off. The ground was saturated with water, and we managed to get our feet wet. Not smart. We didn't, of course, have any dry socks with us. We settled in for the night, Karl in the back seat, and me in the front. I tried the radio again, but couldn't raise anyone. It had cooled off some, but we had a pretty good night under the circumstances.

The next morning, I turned the radio on, and there were some pilots having a conversation. When they finished, I transmitted my numbers, and asked if anyone copied. Yes, they copied. It was Bob, a neighbor from the farm, and a mechanic. They were happy, and very relieved to hear that we were ok. They were flying up and down the glacier looking for us.

Our neighbor had a Cessna 180, and he had been in Delta giving his son some flying lessons the evening before. They said that when I didn't show up by 7:30 pm, they all climbed in the 180 and came out to look for us. They couldn't get very far because of the fog, so they went back to Delta, and tried again in the morning.

The spot where we landed *

I told them we were just over the ridge to the east, but they couldn't get to us because the top of the ridge was still socked in. I told the mechanic what I needed to repair the gear attachment. They said that they would try to get back later to drop us some supplies, and then they headed back to Delta.

The first thing they did when they got back to the hangar was to call the farm and tell them that Karl and I were ok. You can imagine the state of mind that Betty and Karin were in. Karin said that in Germany, when a small plane didn't show up on time, it was because it had crashed. She thought we had crashed and were both dead. Everyone was very happy, and thankful that we were ok.

It was late afternoon when I looked to the north and saw some clear sky. We were both sitting in the plane; maybe they could get in now. Just a couple minutes later, I looked to the east, and saw lights coming up over the ridge. They had done it; here they came!

They flew over low and dropped some boxes out. They circled around and dropped some more stuff. They dropped a six-pack of Pepsi cola, and only one can broke when it hit some rocks. I got on the radio and said, "This is just like Christmas, thanks guys!" Bob radioed back and said, "Oh, you're welcome, I was going to haul this stuff to the dump, but I thought you might be able to use it instead." He had a good sense of humor. We definitely could use it. There were warm dry socks, a big bag of sandwiches, candy bars and other things.

They told us they would be back the next morning so they wanted us to get out first thing and find a place they could land with two Super Cubs. We sure would do that. We put on some dry socks, ate all the sandwiches we could hold, and went to sleep.

The next morning dawned bright and clear. Karl walked about a half mile up the slope and found a place about 400 feet long that was clear of big rocks, and it was solid ground. He came back and told me about it, and we both went back up to wait for the planes. He stood at the top end and I stood at the bottom end. It wasn't long until we heard them coming. They circled a couple of times checking it out and landed.

We all went down to my plane and the mechanic repaired the gear leg attachment. We had to get my plane up the hill to the take-off place. I got in and started the engine. There was a man on each wing pushing, a man walking ahead showing me the way around the rocks and pools of water, and I drove the plane up there. We had to cross the small creek, but that was not a problem. I got the plane in position for take-off, set the brakes, and got out.

We stood around a while, talking about what had happened. After looking around, they were all very surprised I had managed to land where I did without serious damage to the airplane. I just said that I had a lot of help from the Lord.

One of the pilots asked me if I had thought about tuning in to the Automatic Direction Finding (ADF) frequency at Delta, and climbing up out of the fog. Well, I had not thought of that. However, it might have worked. Maybe a more experienced pilot would have known to do that. During flight training, all pilots get a little training on the instruments, but it is not enough to qualify for Instrument Flight Rules (IFR). I was only qualified for Visual Flight Rules (VFR).

In other words, I was only legally qualified to fly when I could see where I was going. Another thing was that I was not familiar enough with the terrain. As far as I knew, had I flown into the fog I might have flown right into the side of a mountain. Also, while taking flight training, you are taught to never, never, never, fly into the clouds! I believe I handled it the only way that was available to me.

*Rescue Crew at the Landing Site ***

We all talked a while longer, and I turned to Karl and said, "Well, Karl, what do you think, shall we fly back to Delta?" He never said a word, just smiled and climbed in the back seat and fastened his seatbelt. We took off with no problem, and I circled around while the other planes got off, and we headed for Delta.

While I was circling around, I noticed that the direction I was going to take when I saw that bright spot in the fog led right into a box canyon. If I had continued into it, we certainly would have crashed — no question about it. I was sure glad that I listened to that inner voice that was screaming, "NO! Don't go there!"

57 Flying to Molly Creek

One caribou season Ed came down and was staying in their cabin across the creek. He hadn't decided yet where he wanted to hunt, and was doing some odds and ends around the cabin. I mentioned to him one day that I was thinking of flying over to Molly Creek, and asked him if he'd like to go along. He said he would, so we went over to the airstrip and I got my plane ready. Molly Creek is northeast of Dry Creek and empties into the Middle Fork of the Forty Mile River. The airstrip is on a ridge-top near Norrell Creek. It's located in Game Management Unit 20E, north of the Tanana River.

I'd heard that Molly Creek was a good place to get caribou, but our intention that day was to just look the place over. I'd heard it was a popular place and that many hunters used it. Soon after we took off from Dry Creek it started to rain, then the wind came up.

Well, that old wind did it to me again! It was raining so hard that I couldn't see forward out of the windscreen, but could only see down out of the side windows. I figured time-wise that we should be close to Molly Creek but I didn't see anything below that looked familiar.

Southeast of Molly Creek about 25 or 30 miles is a place called Mosquito Flats. It's also the origin of the Mosquito Fork of the Forty Mile River. There is a cabin there called Mitchell's Ranch. Well, there we were, happily flying along, expecting any minute to spot Molly Creek, when I looked down out of the window. Mosquito Flats was right below us, and I could see Mitchell's Ranch on the northeast side of the flats so I knew exactly where we were.

I turned to a northwesterly heading. The rain had started to let up, and by the time we got to Molly Creek it had quit altogether so we landed. There were several other planes there, and some of the hunters had gotten caribou. We spent some time looking around and talking with some of the guys. I guess it was true that a lot of people hunted there because one enterprising fellow had set a tent up and was selling coffee and hamburgers. We flew back to Dry Creek, happy that it had all worked out ok.

Caribou Hunt in the Forty Mile Country. *

58 Guardian Angels

Another experience I had, along a little different line, happened in the early 1980's. The Pastor of the Dot Lake Chapel decided to build a new church building. The Chapel by the lake was quite small and on special occasions such as weddings, Easter Sunday, and funerals, a lot of folks had to stand and sometimes they even had to stand outside.

If I remember correctly, the new building was about 24 feet by 40 feet. We used 10 inch, two sided logs that were flattened on the top and bottom but the sides were left round.

The logs were also tongue and grooved to seal the joints between them. Since my trade was carpentry, they asked me to help with the job. Also, a group of people came up from the lower 48 and helped. "Many hands make light work," as the old saying goes.

We put in a full basement with concrete footings and floor and laid up 12" concrete blocks for the basement walls. Everything went well. The folks from "outside" (that's what Alaskans call any place outside of Alaska) stayed until the building was up and the roof framing was finished, and then left for home. They did a great job, and their help was much appreciated.

We used 2" x 6" tongue and groove lumber for the roof boards, with the beveled side down to make the finished ceiling underneath. It was getting late in the fall and it snowed lightly occasionally. One morning Brian and I went down there to work. We had gotten up about eight feet with the roof boards the previous day. It had snowed that night and the roof was covered with an inch or so of the white stuff.

Well, there was *no way* I was getting up on that roof. It was difficult enough on a dry roof, not to mention a snow covered one. Brian stayed and helped, but I went over to the lodge and had some coffee. I hung around there all morning. Brian came over around noon, and we had some lunch.

We went back over there after lunch and checked it out. That morning they had gotten within a few feet of the top and the new roof boards were nice and dry, so I decided I would go up there and help finish it up. When we got up to the last board, it had to be ripped. I gave the guy down below the measurements, and he started sawing them.

While I was standing there waiting I noticed the snow again on the lower part of the roof and decided to sweep it off so the wood would dry out quicker. Someone threw a push broom up to me. The snow was very wet, and I had to slap the broom down on the roof often to knock the snow out of it. I was happily sweeping away, working my way across the roof. What I didn't realize was that when I slapped the broom on the roof to knock the snow out of it, the slushy snow was splattering up on the dry boards that I was walking on.

We had a 2" x 4" fastened along the bottom edge of the roof to catch tools and things that might slip out of our hands. That way they wouldn't fall all the way to the ground. Suddenly, my right foot slipped on that wet roof and in a split second I had fallen and was sliding on my back, head first down the roof. I thought when I got to that 2" x 4", I would grab it to stop my fall. What I hadn't thought of was that by the time my hands got to the 2" x 4", most of my body was already over the edge of the roof.

Jackie was down below sweeping the floor when she heard a "thump" and looked up just in time to see me going down past the window, headfirst. I hit the ground right on the top of my head. It felt like someone hit me on the head with a baseball bat! Then my body hit. There were some small stumps down there and I missed them all, but my back was really hurting.

Folks came running out to help me. They tried to help me get up, but I asked them not to because my back was hurting so bad. My head and the rest of me seemed ok. Paul's wife Martha was a nurse, and she said they should get me to Fairbanks for a checkup. They called the clinic in Delta and told them what had happened. They wanted to get me to the hospital as soon as possible, so Paul asked the ambulance to start out for Dot Lake. He told them he would get me in his truck and start out for Delta. They managed to get me in the back of Paul's pick up and laid me on some blankets. I don't remember where we met the ambulance, but they transferred me and headed for Fairbanks.

An x-ray showed that I had fractured a vertebra in my lower back. They put me in a body cast, from my armpits to my hips. I spent the night in the hospital. It was a very miserable night, I might add. I was aware that I never liked to be in tight places, but I didn't realize that I was claustrophobic. The cast was very tight, and I couldn't even take a deep breath.

I tried to get to sleep. I tried every position adjustment on the bed, but it didn't help. I was getting very frustrated. I rang the bell for the nurse. It was almost midnight, and I still couldn't get to sleep. I told the nurse that she had to get that doctor back in there and cut that thing off me, because I couldn't breathe. She left and came back a little while later with a pill for me to take. I took the pill, and that was the last thing I knew until morning. Before I went home, however, the doctor did cut a hole in the cast about 8" in diameter, so I could take a deep breath when I needed to. That was a big relief.

The only way we could get to our cabin was by walking or riding a snow machine. The doctor told me he didn't want me to do either one, so we had to find a place in Dot Lake to live for a couple of months while my back healed. The whole experience was not pleasant, but it could have been a lot worse.

I had another experience at that same church years later. The first pastor had long since passed on and Paul had become pastor. He was the pastor there for several years, then he and his family moved to North Pole, Alaska. The church was closed for a while for lack of a pastor. In the following years several different "part time" pastors came for short periods of time.

In the late 90's some folks came and opened the church for a couple of years. During that time Larry, the pastor, decided to finish the basement up. He wanted to have some Sunday school rooms down there. He also wanted to build new stairs because the original stairs were narrow and steep. He asked me if I would help him and I said I would be glad to.

One day I was working on an aluminum stepladder and I was three steps up. I started to climb down, but when I moved my right foot the edge of my shoe caught in the groove of the step and threw me off balance. It happened so fast! I hit the concrete floor flat on my back. I lay there for a few seconds. The first thing I noticed was that I didn't hurt anywhere.

Larry wanted to help me up, but I told him no because I had a certain way I had to do it. I got up and we went right back to work. A few minutes later I said, "Hey, Larry, I don't hurt anywhere!" He told me that as he watched me fall it was like slow motion, as if I had just slowly lain down on the floor. How could a person fall flat on his back on a concrete floor from a distance of three feet and not get hurt? Not even a headache? I believe that my guardian angels were there! We thanked God.

59 Copper River Salmon

Back in the 1970's we used to go to Chitina, Alaska for salmon. There was a dip net fishery there on the Copper River. Alaska residents could obtain a permit from Fish and Game for 30 salmon per household. For our family that was plenty. I bought two long handled dip nets, and we went down there to give it a try.

The dip net season opened the 1st of June. We stopped at a gas station on the road to Chitina to fill our tanks up. The elderly native man who owned the station told us that the main salmon run was in May. He said Fish and Game set the opening of the dip net season for June 1st to allow a higher escapement of salmon to get upstream so there would be lots of fish for the next year. That may have been true, but the Copper River is a big river, and I couldn't believe that people with dip nets could hurt the fish population much. However, that's the way it was, and we were glad for the opportunity to get fish.

We were successful, and brought home some nice salmon. The only problem in those days was that the boundary for dip netters was south of O'Brien Creek, and the riverbank there was very steep. There was a narrow place right next to the river where a person could stand to dip, but it was 20 feet or so up to the trail. It was quite difficult for me to get up there with my fish. We went there several times, and always got fish, but it got to be more work than fun so we stopped going for a while.

One time Ed and I went down and hired a guy with a boat to take us downstream a ways. He dropped us off on the east bank of the river. It was a good spot, and there were only a couple of other people there. The water was about three feet deep. I was afraid I wouldn't be able to stand up in the swift current, so Ed did all the work. He had waders on, and had to walk out in the river a ways to dip. He did well and we came home with plenty of fish.

Betty shows off salmon ready for canning

While we were building the new Dot Lake chapel, one of the men who came up from the lower 48 was an electrician. He and Paul got an idea to build a fish wheel. I don't know who invented it, but the fish wheel is a wonderful piece of equipment. The current of the river operates it. Fish wheels have two large wire baskets opposite each other, and two board paddles opposite the baskets. The river current pushes against the wooden paddles and the baskets, and turns the fish wheel.

There is a large wooden box on the side, and when the baskets scoop up the fish, they slide out the side of the basket into the box. Ingenious! All a guy has to do is take the rope off that's holding the baskets and it starts working. Then he just goes down and checks the box occasionally, and takes out the fish. They built their fish wheel out of electrical conduit. They did a great job; it was light and easy to move around, and it worked great.

Salmon are amazing creatures. I'm sure most people know how they return every year to the place where they were hatched to spawn, and the cycle continues, year after year. I don't remember how far it is from the Bering Sea to our area, but I'm sure it's a thousand miles or more. Those salmon come all that way up the

Yukon River to the Tanana River, and up the Tanana to their spawning places.

Paul got the idea to put his fish wheel in the Tanana River just upstream from its confluence with the Johnson River. We could drive down the Johnson River bed all the way to the Tanana so that made it easy. We dragged the fish wheel a hundred yards or so upstream and tied it off to a tree. It worked really well.

I got the idea to build a small smoker, and smoke some of the salmon. I had never tried that before, but smoked salmon is good stuff. I built it about 2½ feet high and 18 inches square. It had an opening at the top for the smoke to escape, and an opening at the bottom for the fire pot. I cut the bottom off of a 5-gallon kerosene can, about 6 inches high, for the fire pot. It had a door on the front side, and I put in wooden dowels about 3 inches apart to hang the strips of fish on near the top. I went down to the river and cut some alder sticks up to 1" in diameter and about 10 inches long. I would use dry sticks to get the green alder burning.

Betty made a marinade and we soaked the pieces of fish in that overnight. The next morning, I hung the strips of fish in the smoker, lit the fire, and shut the door. If I remember correctly, I let them smoke for about ten hours, adding green alder sticks as needed. These were silver salmon — maybe not quite as good as reds — but still very good. I was very pleased at the way it turned out.

Virgil had gotten acquainted with a native man who had a fish wheel in the Copper River, fifty miles or so upstream from Chitina. He told Virgil that he could use it, so he and his wife Juanita, and Betty and I went down there one year. We had a pickup truck with a camper on it, and we camped out there for three days. We let the fish wheel run day and night. We would go down and check it several times during the day, and of course, first thing every morning. It worked really great. Virgil and I cleaned and cut the fish up into chunks, and Betty and Juanita canned them right there on the spot. That is the way to do it...the easiest way to fish that I know of. Maybe not as much fun as fishing with a rod, but certainly much more productive. So, all we had to do when we got home was put the jars of fish down in the root cellar and wait for our first fish dinner.

All of the rivers in Alaska are dangerous, and a person has to figure out the safest way to use them. It is not always possible to do it this way, but one time when Ed and I went to Chitina for salmon, he was able to back his truck right up close to the river. They had moved the boundary of the dip net fishery farther upstream, and we didn't have to go down to O'Brien creek to dip anymore.

Ed put his waders on and got out a long rope. He tied one end of the rope to his truck and the other end around his waist—a very smart move! If a person with chest high waders should lose his balance and fall down in the river, his waders could fill up with water. He would most likely not be able to get back on his feet, and could be swept downstream to his doom. It has happened before. Ed was able to wade out and do some dip netting, knowing that if he did slip and fall, he could pull himself back to shore with the rope. A very comforting thought.

60 When Life Hands You Lemons…Use Sticks and Wire

One winter, Dick and I decided to try to get to Fish Lake on our snow machines. It is approximately eighteen miles the way we would have to go. The snow was deep that year. We left Dry Creek and went up Squeaky's trail. Near the top of the plateau was a place where a small creek spread out and froze over. It was a difficult place to get over. Dick was leading and he got over it just fine, but I guess I didn't have enough speed as I hit the ice.

About halfway across it, I spun out and my machine started sliding sideways. It hit some brush that was sticking up out of the ice and flipped over, throwing me off. Well, I managed to grab a ski, so the machine and I went sliding down the hill. I hung on to that ski! Wherever that machine was going to end up, I was going to be there with it when it stopped! It wasn't too bad; we probably slid a hundred feet or so and got stopped by some brush. I managed to get the machine over on some snow, got a good start, and made it up over the top.

When we got over to Berry Creek Ridge we stopped to look around. Over on the far side of Berry Creek, we saw a large moose. Looking through our binoculars, we discovered that it was a bull. He had already shed his antlers, but the area where they had been attached was, we guessed, close to four inches in diameter—a large bull. I surmised that it could have been the same one Brian and I had seen the year before on our trip to this area.

We had to go down several hundred feet to get to a place where we could cross Berry Creek because the hillsides rose up very steeply from the creek. We crossed, and then climbed up again on the east side. It was several miles up and around the west end of the high ridge, and then we turned east along the base of the ridge toward Fish Lake.

Dick is a good rider, and he was in the lead. We did ok for another mile or so, but we finally had to give it up. The snow was just too deep, so we kept getting bogged down. We got our machines turned around and started back. Even though we were running in the track we had just made, it was still soft and difficult.

In deep, soft snow you have to stand on the running boards and continually rock the machine back and forth to keep it going. We had to climb a hill to get up out of the place where we got bogged down. I was really horsing my machine around to keep moving forward, and suddenly my handlebars broke off. There was about a four inch piece of the steering tube left on the handlebars, and it broke off about three inches above the bracket that held the steering tube to the frame.

Well! Here we were about ten miles from home. What to do? I always carried a pair of six-inch vise-grips in my snow machine, as well as some wire, and a small saw for cutting brush. I clamped the vise-grips on the steering tube as tight as I could. I cut a piece of alder an inch in diameter and about sixteen inches long and wired it to the vise-grips. Of course the throttle was still attached to the handlebars, so I had to operate the throttle with my right hand, and steer with my left. I finally got the hang of it, and we made it back home just fine, with no more problems.

The next day I got an idea how to fix it. I found a round solid iron bar that just fit inside the steering tube, and I cut it to ten inches long. I drilled three holes in the tube on the handlebars and three holes on the lower steering tube that was fastened to the steering mechanism. I drilled them all the way through, so I had six holes on each one. I took the machine over to my neighbor, who had an electric welder. He slipped the iron bar down inside the tube and spot-welded one of the holes. He put the handlebars over the iron bar and spot-welded the rest of the holes. It was just like new, maybe better!

61 Snow Machine Fun

Another time, Dick, Billy and I went up on the plateau to just tear around and have some fun. It's a wide-open country up there, and you can go as fast as you want to, or at least, as fast as your machine will go. In those days the snow machines weren't as fast as they are today. Fifty miles an hour was top speed for mine.

It was lot of fun, and we saw some wildlife as well. We saw a herd of 15 or 20 caribou. They were climbing a steep hill. In deep snow they walk single file to make it easier. It was quite a sight.

We played around for a while, and decided that instead of coming back down Squeaky's trail we would go around to the west and come down the old horse trail. That was the first trail used by hunters with horses and mules. It was a more gradual climb, and easier on the animals. We had never been on that trail with snow machines before and didn't really know what to expect, but we decided to give it a try. The first surprise came when we broke over the edge and started down.

The first couple hundred yards was hard, wind packed snow. We really got going fast, and when we tried to use our brakes, the track would lock up, and we would start sliding sideways. That wasn't good, so we let up on the brakes and really started flying down the hill. Farther down we managed to get over into some soft snow and get slowed down.

A little later we came to the edge of a very steep place. We got off our machines, and walked over to check it out to see if we could make down. It wasn't straight down, but it was very steep. It was about a hundred yards or so down to where it leveled off. Dick was in the lead again and said, "It doesn't look too bad." Then he started his machine and disappeared over the edge. It seemed like a long time before he showed up again, way down at the bottom. He waved to us, and I was next in line, so I started my machine and went over the edge. Well, I'll tell you, that was some ride! What a thrill! I made it down ok, and Dick and I watched as Billy popped over the edge. This all went on before Billy had his heart attack, so it didn't bother him. But when he popped over the edge and started down, he said it felt like his heart skipped a beat or two.

The only other obstacle was that when we got down lower and dropped down into the creek bottom, we came to two large boulders. It was a good thing that the snow was deep. The creek banks were very steep and we wouldn't be able to get our machines back up out of it, so we had to go straight ahead. The snow was deep enough so that with some lifting and tugging we were able to get our machines in between the rocks. Everything worked out, and we had another fun day.

62 An Unexpected Catch

I want to tell you about an interesting incident that happened on our trapline. Jason and I had gotten our line cut from Plateau Lake to Sears Creek. Sometimes we would go north to the old pipeline right of way, then east to Sears Creek and around that way, and sometimes we went up the East Fork and around, for a change of scenery.

This morning we headed up the East Fork. Three miles up, our line crossed the creek and turned east up a wide valley. The upper end of the valley is quite open with small spruce trees and muskeg. As we approached one of our sets, we could see that we had something in a trap, but couldn't yet tell what is was.

When we got closer we could see that there was a golden eagle in one of the traps. That was a first; we had never caught an eagle before. He had seen or smelled the bait, and had come down to check it out, and put his little foot right in a number four jump trap. I asked Jason to find a forked stick so he could hold the eagle's head down while I got the trap off his leg. As you know, eagles have a large, hooked beak, and I didn't want him pecking on me.

This type of trap has a very strong spring. A man can set them by hand, but I usually used a C-clamp. I would definitely have to use the clamp today. Jason couldn't find a forked stick so this job might be a little difficult. I got my clamp out and started talking to the bird in a soft, low tone as I walked slowly around to where I could get at the trap. I told him that I wasn't going to hurt him; I was going to get that thing off his leg so he could be free again.

I was really surprised. He didn't struggle to get away. He just lay still, and looked up at me with that big yellow eye. Maybe he somehow knew that I was trying to help him. I kept talking to him and reached down slowly, put the clamp on the trap and started to turn the screw. As soon as he felt the pressure of the trap jaws lighten, he pulled his leg out and took off, half running, half flying to get away. We replaced the trap with a clean one. When we finished that job, we looked around, and he was gone. We never saw him again. That was a strong trap, but it didn't break his leg. I'm sure he wasn't hurt at all, and he is still soaring the skies, living a normal life. It was a thrill to be so close to one of those magnificent birds.

Another time, I was coming down the East Fork on my trapline. I was only a mile or so from our cabin, but it had been a long day. I was getting tired, so I shut my machine off and got off to stretch out a bit. One of the most populous furbearers we have in Alaska is the marten. They, wolverines, and weasels are all in the same family. They are meat eaters, and they can be fierce if cornered. In the winter, weasels turn white and are called ermine. Now you ladies know that ermine coats are made of weasels!

There are three sizes of weasels. The smallest, called a least weasel, is only about 6 inches tall. Sometimes you can see them sitting up like groundhogs do. I was standing there looking around, when I heard snarling and growling behind me. I turned around to see what was going on.

There was a washed out place in the creek bank with no snow in it, and there was one of those little white squirts standing there, growling at me and acting like he was going to eat me up. It was really funny, and I just had to laugh right out loud at his antics. He didn't back off, either. When I got back on my machine and left, he was still standing there growling at me.

63 Living off the Land

Well, I've told a lot of stories of our life here on the East Fork: lots of excitement and adventure. On the other hand, there were a lot of "normal" days too! Cutting firewood, picking wild berries, and Betty spends a lot of time in the greenhouse and garden.

In the spring of 1975, after our bear hunt, we started clearing the area that would be our garden and a future greenhouse. We cleared an area approximately 30 feet by 50 feet. There were 18 birch trees that would have to be removed, and a few spruce trees. Some of the birch trees were double, and there was one that had three trees growing out of the same stump.

Breaking ground for the garden, 1975

I went to Fairbanks and bought a case of dynamite, some fuses, caps, and a tool for inserting the fuse and cap in the dynamite, and to crimp the caps to the fuse, and some plastic tape to hold the fuse and dynamite together. I had seen dynamite used before, and had a little knowledge of how to do it, but I had never done it myself. However, that was the only means I had of getting the stumps out, so I had to give it a try.

Brian and I went to work on it. First, we cut the trees down and into firewood length, about 18 inches, and stacked it on the woodpile. I had a steel bar that I used to punch holes under the stumps to put the dynamite in. I cut the fuse about three feet long, and that gave us lots of time to run and hide behind a tree. I didn't know how much dynamite I should use, so first I tried a half stick, and all it did was vibrate the ground a little. Also, after the first try, I discovered that there was still frost in the ground and that was making the job a little more difficult. The next time I used two sticks and that worked well. On the three-tree stump I tried three sticks. That only loosened it up a little so I put another charge of four sticks under it and that did the job.

There were lots of roots left in the ground after the stumps were all removed, and we went after it with mattocks, hoes and rakes, and got it leveled off and ready for planting.

Our new rototiller, 1976

I had worked out at Ft. Greely in 1979. We remodeled some buildings and replaced the windows. I was able to buy the old windows at a good price, so I got some of them, anticipating that I would build a greenhouse someday. In 1983, Doug and his wife came for a visit, and he helped me build a 16' x 20' greenhouse.

I built planters along each side about 3' wide, and a 5' x 8' one in the center of the greenhouse. I put a barrel stove in the north end. The folks at the farm gave us some started tomato plants and Betty transplanted them in the greenhouse. She also got bell pepper plants and some flowers. We bought some seeds in town too. Between the greenhouse and garden, she produced a lot of good food!

One of our favorite berries is the low-bush cranberry. They are plentiful every year and are delicious. While not a true cranberry (also known as Lingonberries) they are a great replacement.

Alaska "low-bush cranberries"

In the early years we picked soapberries too. We read in one of our books that you could whip them up, put a little sweetener in it, and it would be just like whipped cream. We tried in once. It was okay, but we didn't really care for it, so we didn't do it again. We also made birch syrup one time. It was a reddish color and wasn't too bad, but was a far cry from good old maple syrup, so we didn't do that again either.

Another thing we tried was fireweed leaf salad. That was very good. One time, though, Betty put some blue bell leaves in it, and they made it taste like fish, so we left them out the next time.

Wild Bluebells

Fireweed flowers along our road (wild rhubarb in the background)

Back in Michigan we had morel mushrooms, and we wondered if there were any in Alaska. There are many varieties of mushrooms in Alaska, but we don't bother with them because we aren't familiar enough with them and we don't want to take a chance of getting sick. We do know the morels though, and we have found some of those. I don't know why, but they have disappeared from around our place. You can still find them in some areas after a forest fire goes through.

You definitely want to know what you're doing, if you're going after mushrooms. Some years back they found an old "sourdough" dead in his cabin. He was sitting at the table with a plate full of mushrooms. If anyone should know mushrooms, it should have been him, but somehow he must have gotten some bad ones, and they did him in.

There are some other wild berries that we have in abundance in Alaska. I've already mentioned low bush cranberries. There are also high bush cranberries, raspberries and blueberries. In some areas you can also find wild strawberries. There are also cloudberries, and many others, but we don't find many of those in our area.

Of course we have wild roses in abundance and use all phases of the rose. The petals make a beautiful pink colored jelly that is delicious.

Alaskan Wild Rose

Betty uses the rose hips before they are ripe to make a jelly that reminds us of apple jelly. The ripe rosehips make good fruit leathers and even a meat sauce or ketchup substitute.

Rose hips are the fruit of the rose, formed after the petals fall off.

I like all the Alaskan berries, but my favorite is wild blueberries. I like to have Betty make jam from them. She puts it in small jars, and I'll take one jar and loosen the top a little and let it set for a week or two. It gets a little "tangy." Then I take a piece of Betty's warm fry bread, slice it partway open and put in some butter and some of that blueberry jam. You have never tasted anything so delicious. It is so good! My mouth is watering right now, just thinking about it.

One year I was up in the Fortymile country hunting caribou. I don't know where the caribou were, but they weren't anywhere around where I was. I noticed that the blueberries were ripe so I spent some time picking them. If I remember correctly, I brought home three gallons, not counting the half gallon or so that I ate while picking them. Berry picking and hunting mushrooms was one of our family pastimes back in Michigan, and we really enjoy berry picking (and eating) in Alaska too.

64 Conclusion

The year is 2013. I'm sitting here on the deck of our log cabin on the East Fork of Dry Creek. It's the 5th day of February. The temperature is eight degrees above zero. You may think that it's too cold to be sitting outside. It's a little nippy, but I'm dressed warmly and I'm comfortable. My dog, Blue, and I are having coffee and biscuits. I drink the coffee, and he eats the biscuits. We started this last summer. I was having my coffee out here on my deck one morning, and I gave him a couple of those small "doggie biscuits." We all know how easily habits are formed, and now he thinks that every time I have coffee, he should have a biscuit. He's even beginning to think that every time Betty has a cup of coffee, he should have a biscuit!

Blue is an Australian Shepherd, blue merle color phase, hence his name. His formal name is Little Boy Blue, but we call him Buddy most of the time. My family gave him to me for my 80th birthday. He turned five years old on April 20th, 2013. And me? Well, I'm getting older too...

Blue is very smart, and is a good watchdog. Nothing moves or makes a noise around here that he doesn't see or hear. If he barks and we can't see anything, it's probably the scent of something coming in on the wind that has alerted him.

We often have moose in the yard, and I just noticed that one walked through sometime last night, not more than six feet from the deck. Also, we have rabbits, foxes, coyotes, and bears in the summertime, and during the migration season even caribou, and occasionally a lone wolf wanders through.

Our cabin is about a half mile from the base of Macomb Plateau. At that point the terrain rises steeply for about 1500 feet, then it rises more gradually to the higher elevations of the Alaska Range. One of the most exciting times of the year for us is when the sun shines in our front windows around the end of January. I realize that may sound a bit silly to some folks, but because we are so close to the mountains we lose the sun around Thanksgiving and don't see it again until the end of January.

After the short days and the long dark nights of December and January, that sunshine is a very welcome sight. The sun first appears in what we call the East Fork Notch. It is a dip in the ridgeline where the East Fork Creek comes down out of the mountains. At first, it is only in the notch for a few minutes, but every day it gets a little higher until about ten or twelve days later it rises above the ridge line and moves west along the ridge for a couple of hours before it disappears again behind the higher mountains. Then it continues to rise higher in the sky until May, June, and July, when we have almost 24 hours of daylight.

The Macomb Plateau in summer, as seen from the Alaska Highway

This morning it is shining down in its full strength through the frost covered birch trees, and reflecting off the snowflakes on the ground. It's a true winter wonderland. If one looks carefully, under certain light conditions, you can see colors reflecting off the snowflakes. The most common colors that I have noticed are green, blue, amber, and rose color. If you move your head side to side, some colors disappear and others come into view. I continue to marvel at the beauty of God's creation.

Our cabin in the early years

Well, I've had a lot of experiences these last forty years, and I guess I can say they were all good, since I survived them all. It was fun having an airplane. It fulfilled an inner desire I'd had since I was a boy. But the desire and the longing for the wilderness that brought me to Alaska is just as strong today as it was the day I left Michigan. This wonderful place has been our home for the last forty years, and counting. I sincerely believe that here is where my destiny has always been.

Even though we're getting older, this place in the wilderness is where our hearts desire to be as long as we are able. I appreciate Diana, Pam and Brian, who came with us, helped build our cabin, and shared a few years of their lives with us, until they all struck out to find their own way through life. Brian now lives in Florida with his wife, a son and a daughter. Diana has settled in Delta Junction, after trying out several different locations in Alaska. She has two daughters. One lives in North Dakota and another in Ohio. Pam lives in Fairbanks, and she has one daughter who lives in Anchorage.

Current photo of our home

The "Haybarn," as seen from our front deck

I am not able to get around on the trapline or hunt like I used to, but I have a storehouse full of good memories. Sometimes when I'm sitting out on the deck having coffee and biscuits with my dog Blue, my mind wanders off to some past hunting trip, some experience I had on the trapline, or good times we've had with family and neighbors.

I haven't, however, given up on hunting. Maybe this will be the year, as I'm sitting out here on my deck having coffee and some of Betty's delicious cookies, that a big bull moose will come along, and give me the opportunity to unlimber my big .69 caliber flintlock rifle and get us some moose steaks. Ah, life is good here on the East Fork!

Bob and Betty in their home with Blue, 2014

From the publisher...

Thank you for purchasing this book. If you enjoyed what you've read, please consider leaving an honest review on Amazon. It would be greatly appreciated!

Made in the USA
Middletown, DE
30 September 2018